Thinking of...

Backing Up Data In Your Business?

Ask the Smart Questions

By Guy Bunker and Gareth Fraser-King

First Published in 2010 by Smart Questions Limited, Fryern House, 125 Winchester Road, Chandlers Ford, Hampshire, SO53 2DR, UK
Web: *www.Smart-Questions.com* (including ordering of printed and electronic copies, extended book information, community contributions and details on charity donations)
Email: *info@Smart-Questions.com* (for customer services, bulk order enquiries, reproduction requests et al)

A catalogue record for this book is available from the British Library.

ISBN 978-1-907453-04-5

SQ-23-169-001-001

Smart Questions™ Philosophy

Smart Questions is built on 4 key pillars, which set it apart from other publishers:

1. *Smart people want Smart Questions not Dumb Answers*
2. *Domain experts are often excluded from authorship, so we are making writing a book simple and painless*
3. *The community has a great deal to contribute to enhance the content*
4. *We donate a percentage of revenue to a charity voted for by the authors and community. It is great marketing, but it is also the right thing to do*

www.Smart-Questions.com

Reviews

As many organizations are learning these days, backup and in particular recovery have become more challenging tasks as the number and complexity of systems in the organization continue to rise. This book provides a clear and comprehensive explanation of how an organization should approach their backups and how to avoid the pitfalls which can lead to potential loss of valuable systems and data.

Lewis McMahon, Owner, Storage Online Ltd

Although backup and recovery seems as simple as copying bits *from point to point, it is far more challenging to implement properly when considering the details involved. This book captures the decades of backup and storage experience that Gareth Fraser-King and Guy Bunker have in the industry and make them ideally suited to provide the insights and questions you should be asking of your backup vendor or provider.*

Pat Hanavan, Vice President, Symantec Corporation

This book will be an invaluable resource to our customers. Understanding the right questions to ask has helped us provide the right solution for the problems they have.

Wayne Cockerill, Managing Director, Aindale BMS Ltd

We had looked at backup, but the more we looked into it, the more it seemed to be a real minefield. Using the book we were able to approach our technical partner, Aindale, who quickly helped us find the right solution.

Ian Jackson, Director, Compact Software.

As data becomes the lifeblood of even small and medium sized organizations, the need for information continuity is even more important. Being able to ask the right questions gives these organizations an advantage over those who choose to work without informed help.

Clive Longbottom, Service Director, Business Process Analysis, Quocirca Ltd

I know it sounds awful, but when I had my laptop nicked I experienced grief for the first time in my life. Gareth helped me as much as he could after the event but the horse had bolted. He couldn't believe I hadn't backed up my data. Nor can I now. This book makes absolutely essential reading for anyone – even me, if I could read.

Math Priest, Rock God, Entrepreneur, Radio Producer and the Drummer from Dodgy

Authors

Guy Bunker

Dr. Guy Bunker is an Independent Security Consultant, having worked at Symantec (formerly VERITAS) for more than a decade, where he was a Distinguished Engineer and responsible for, among other things, Symantec's Utility Computing and Cloud Strategies. He has been involved with backup for 14+ years, from being a developer to designing and installing backup systems for customers.

Guy is an active member of ENISA (European Network and Information Security Agency), The Enterprise Privacy Group and the Jericho Forum. Guy is a regular presenter at many conferences, including RSA Europe, InfoSec and StorageExpo. He is frequently quoted in the press and on television and radio.

Guy has authored a number of books and his latest on data loss prevention, "Data Leaks For Dummies", was published by John Wiley and Sons in March 2009.

Guy holds a PhD in Artificial Neural Networks from King's College London, several patents and is a Chartered Engineer with the IET.

Gareth Fraser-King

Gareth Fraser-King is a IT marketing veteran, the last ten years with Symantec (formally VERITAS) before Symantec he was at Sybase. In the far distant past he has worked as an IT analyst both client-side and agency analysts, with extensive experience in infrastructure IT, producing high level messaging, white papers, articles, presentations, and marketing deliverables. In addition he is a technical author for John Wiley & Sons, Inc with two books: "Data Lifecycles: Managing Data for Strategic Advantage" & "Data Leaks For Dummies".

He has worked extensively across EMEA in technical support, product marketing, technical authoring, business development and quality management. Acknowledged by his customers and colleagues as a valued member of a team that understands business requirements across international markets, he has the ability to take complex product solutions and ensure that they can be understood by all – from the sales force to customers, from CEOs to IT administrators. He can capture the essence of new products and features and explain them in simple and memorable ways, tying the technology to business problems and solutions.

Table of Contents

Acknowledgements

Guy would like to thank his long suffering wife, Susanna and their daughter Veryan for putting up with his strange writing habits. He would also like to thank his four legged writing companions; Archie, Frank and Harry whose attempts to help have made for a better manuscript!

He would also like to thank all his friends, colleagues and customers for their valuable input into this book as well as being the source for the stories and anecdotes.

Gareth would like to dedicate this book to his horribly talented multi-tasking wife, Elaine; her only error was to mistake him for someone nice.

Gareth would like to thank his faithful hound Frank (if you want to be part of this writing team you need to get a black Lab and name him Frank) and the four not so small people who live in the same house, Alice, Ellen, Finnian and Viola (Lolly) who took a reasonable stab at keeping the noise levels down whilst he was working.

Foreword

When I started out in IT, which is many more years ago that I care to remember, there was only one thing that was important to me – the applications. Backup was something that we didn't think about. Systems crashed and we ran around trying to get them back up and running while the users complained– but it was a small company and we didn't really understand what IT infrastructure was all about.

Time has moved on, I've moved jobs a few times and the world has moved on as well. IT is now the cornerstone of our business and like almost every business out there, it needs to be up-and-running 24x7, to paraphrase Gene Kranz *failure is not an option.*

Formula 1 today is all about the data, ok, so the driver is pretty important as well, but without data they wouldn't have a car! Our business is to win races and the F1 championship and at the heart of this is our intellectual property, our data.

Backup is our first and last line of defense and is vital in the IT environment. First line as we know everything is backed up on a regular basis, and last line, because if everything went wrong, we know we could go back to our last set of backups and get going again - quickly.

Exponential data growth and a broader range of data being used to support critical business operations have only increased the focus on backup. The Renault F1 Team is seeing data growth in line with predictions from IDC of around 60% per year. New technologies such as our Computational Fluid Dynamic center which model the cars and their performance before they are built produce vast quantities of information that is essential to the efficient development of the cars. Car design isn't a one off, changes to various parts happens throughout the year and even for different circuits. Historical data is required to for the simulations as well as for direct comparisons with different components under different conditions. Never underestimate the usefulness of historical data!

All our data is backed up and stored safely... just in case.

Prior to 2000, the Renault F1 Team IT organization was focused on maintaining the organization's manufacturing, computer-aided design (CAD) systems and UNIX based workstations as these were seen as the critical components of our IT environment. In 2001 the Renault F1 Team was determined to win the FIA Formula One World Championship – and IT was to be the cornerstone. You might think of Renault F1 as being a big company, back then it wasn't – it was a small business and IT shad to fight for budget. It's not that different today, we still only have a few hundred employees and despite winning a couple of championships, budget discussions are just as tough as ever... and we still only produce 4 cars a year!

Before we started to reinvest and move the infrastructure into the 21st Century we looked at what we couldn't do without and it all came down to data. Intellectual property, design data and race data formed the backbone of the Renault F1 Team's drive to a F1 Championship.

Backup was (and still is) our most cost effective data protection solution. We started with a simple backup solution and backup policies; they grew over time with our environment in order to ensure continuous and timely access to information. This was both in the data center as well as within the travelling IT infrastructure we installed in the trackside garages at every race – beaming the data back to base. Understanding the end goal and getting everyone on the same page proved extremely important to the successful implementation of our consolidated and consistent backup solution. Justifying budget for an underlying service such as backup versus a new server is tough – unless you have lost time and data to a downed system – which we had.

I've known both Gareth and Guy for several years, between them they have over 30 years experience in backup and recovery and you won't find a couple of more boring backup geeks around. Backup has saved my bacon more than once, sometimes very small issues such as a lost laptop and sometimes larger ones like entire servers. We had an incident where a small plane came down in a field near the data center and a what-if disaster question was asked by the board, *"what-if it had hit the data center?" - The answer was, "well we have a complete backup which would get us back up and running and keep us in business"*, but we still reviewed our disaster recovery plans

I would suggest you take a look at this book. I wish I had something like this back when we started to take IT and backup seriously. Knowing what you don't know is tough and so understanding some of the right questions to ask is great, it would have saved me time (and therefore money) to have had a head start on the whole process. Backup technology continues to move at quite a pace and having read this book, there are still some smart questions I need to ask.

Graeme Hackland,

Chief Information Officer, Renault F1 Team

Who should read this book?

People like you and me

This book has been written for anyone who has data that needs to be protected. It is aimed at all those who know that the information they create and store on their computers is important, they have heard of backup but aren't too sure what to do next. They have no doubt heard horror stories of lost data and failed backups and so have tended to use the 'cross your fingers and hope that nothing goes wrong' backup strategy in the past but now want something a little more reliable.

While this book will be useful to larger businesses, the chances are they will already have a backup strategy and solution in place. This is really meant for you, if you have a smaller business – the small to medium size business, SMB. If you don't have a backup solution then this book will help you get started and if you do have a solution then this book will help when you need to review or replace the one you have.

This book is intended to be a catalyst for action aimed at a range of people inside and outside your organization. Here are just a few, and why it is relevant to them.

Chief Executive Officer / Managing Director / Owner

In an SMB, you probably wear several hats, but the one thing for sure is that the buck finally stops with you and you need to ensure that the business stays up and running come rain or shine – efficiently. Lost data could be more than an inconvenience; it could spell disaster for the company. Backup is not an option in today's world; it is a necessity whether you are a one-man-band or a huge multi-national. Putting a backup strategy together and implementing it can remove unnecessary pressures – allowing you to do what you do best… making money and keeping the company growing.

Chief Operations Officer / Chief Information Officer / Owner of IT

Once a company gets to a particular size in terms of IT equipment, it then becomes a role in the business to look after it. These days' people aren't so worried about the computers themselves as they are relatively cheap, it's the data that's important. Understanding just where all this data is and how to best keep it safe is a vital piece of the puzzle.

People Who Have Data They Can't Afford To Lose

You use a computer and you (hopefully) do work of value to the business on it – importantly, you don't want to have to redo it over and over should the machine break down. You are at the sharp end of a failed computer and so have the most to lose should there not be an efficient backup environment in the company.

Software Vendors and Resellers Who Are Selling Backup or Backup Services

Perhaps you are a backup guru inside a company who is selling backup products and / or services. If so, then this book is also for you. Understanding some of the questions your customers are going to ask you will help you put together a better solution for them. As a guru, you will know the ins-and-outs of backup, the real nitty-gritty and it is often the simple questions that are overlooked. Not because you don't know the answer – but because you assume that everyone knows it!

Take a look through and try to match questions to the customer you are going to see – then you can be prepared with appropriate answers and pre-empt some of them.

How to use this book

This book is intended to be the catalyst for action. We hope that the ideas and examples inspire you to act. So, do whatever you need to do to make this book useful. Go to our website and email colleagues the e-book summary. Use Post-it notes, write on it, rip it apart, or read it quickly in one sitting. Whatever works for you. We hope this becomes your most dog-eared book.

Clever clogs – skip to the questions

OK, so some of you will know all about backup, or at least have an idea about why it's important and why on the face of it, it is simple and yet when you start to dig into the details it becomes devilishly complicated. You therefore might want to skip the first few chapters and go straight to Chapter 4 where the structure of Smart Questions is explained.

But before you go, please read "Getting Involved" on the next page. You can always come back to Chapters 1-3 later.

Getting Involved

The Smart Questions community

There may be questions that we should have asked but didn't. Or specific questions which may be relevant to your situation, but not everyone in general. Go to the website for the book and post the questions. You never know, they may make it into the next edition of the book. That is a key part of the Smart Questions Philosophy.

Send us your feedback

We love feedback. We prefer great reviews, but we'll accept anything that helps take the ideas further. We welcome your comments on this book.

We'd prefer email, as it's easy to answer and saves trees. If the ideas worked for you, we'd love to hear your success stories. Maybe we could turn them into 'Talking Heads'-style video or audio interviews on our website, so others can learn from you. That's one of the reasons why we wrote this book. So talk to us.

feedback@Smart-Questions.com

Got a book you need to write?

Maybe you are a domain expert with knowledge locked up inside you. You'd love to share it and there are people out there desperate for your insights. But you don't think you are an author and don't know where to start. Making it easy for you to write a book is part of the Smart Questions Philosophy.

Let us know about your book idea, and let's see if we can help you get your name in print.

potentialauthor@Smart-Questions.com

Short History of Backup and Why It Is Needed

Those who cannot remember the past are condemned to repeat it

Santayana (Philosopher, 1863 – 1952)

In the beginning...

WHEN the first computer was created; little did anyone know just how ubiquitous they would become or how much of a headache they could be. Shortly after the first computer was switched on, it broke… and so the need for backup was born.

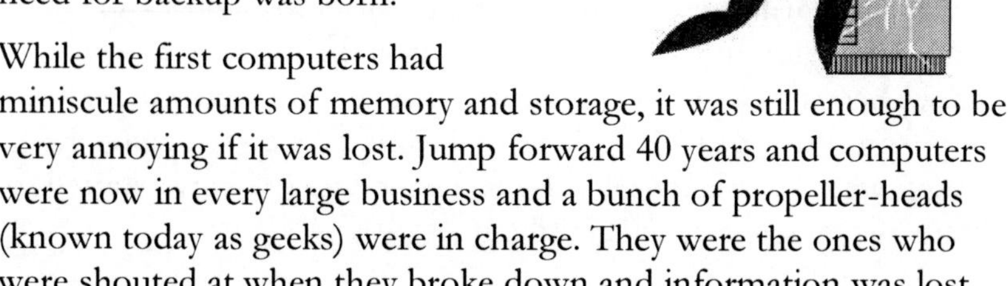

While the first computers had miniscule amounts of memory and storage, it was still enough to be very annoying if it was lost. Jump forward 40 years and computers were now in every large business and a bunch of propeller-heads (known today as geeks) were in charge. They were the ones who were shouted at when they broke down and information was lost.

Backup: The early years

While the larger mainframe computers did have backup applications, they tended to be for the one mainframe – not the

10s, 100s or 1000s of smaller computers that existed. Those systems were backed up with some custom scripts (sets of computer commands) which basically copied the data from the hard disk to a tape. Through the magic of Ethernet connectivity on the local area network (LAN), the administrator could run this command remotely but they didn't have that many tape drives and you still had to run around to change tapes.

Backup: The next generation

Obviously the inefficiencies of not enough tape drives and having to run around was not going to last for long and so the first commercial backup products were born. The idea was simple, package up the scripts, put in place some scheduling mechanisms so you could run the backups at night and be able to route data from one computer to another which had a tape drive on it.

Tapes and tape drives are a curious beast – they run most efficiently when the data is sent to them at an optimal rate, known as streaming. If the data is too slow, then the tape drive spends it's time running the tape back and forwards to find out where the tape should be to have the next bit written. Obviously if there are a lot of systems then one tape won't cut it and so tape libraries came about – these could hold thousands of tapes and several tape drives which could be run simultaneously.

As mainframe computer systems were making the transition from one single massive machine to a range of smaller, more specific, systems the industry gave IT managers a right royal headache … how could they manage these complex environments? At this time backup administrators /system administrators would backup during off hours and the weekends. But as the world got smaller and we began to work longer hours to the point where our virtual shop front was open 24x7 IT needed to find a way to reduce the backup window dramatically. To make matters worse we started to create bucket loads of data (and it goes on).

The data was no longer on a mainframe in the data center; Open Systems ensured that there were hundreds or thousands of servers to add to the copious quantities of workstations across multiple locations – all of which now had business data on them. If backup was tough before, it became really hard now. A new breed of backup was born, centralizing the management of the distributed backups. Open Systems (and the PC) introduced another problem – platform proliferation – each with its own backup solution! The introduction of Application Programming Interfaces (APIs) and standardization helped to integrate backup and recovery functionality across the entire IT estate and provide IT with a simplified and easy-to-manage backup solution.

But speeds were still a problem – tape is all well and good but it takes a good deal of time to recover the tape... especially if you had to go and get it from the offsite vault, bring it to the site, put it in the drive etc. etc. Around about 2000 we worked out that backup have very little to do with backup and everything to do with restore (or retrieval). The three tiered architecture incorporating disk based backup, LAN-free backup, bare-metal machine recovery and VTL (Virtual Tape Library) backup speeded up the whole process.

With technologies such as de-duplication and integrated archiving we are far away from the giddy days of the first backup solutions. Data protection is much more than simple siloed backup processes managing the data stored on single machines. The internet and the increase in unstructured data created by media rich applications (music and the like) has created the need to make sense of all this stuff we have to store and backup. Data growth is big and the only people who ever ask or demand that stuff is deleted are the lawyers – for legal reasons. Left to our own devices, we would all keep everything, forever... just-in-case. If data growth continues at the current rate within a few years it will be doubling every few weeks. So the growth simply doesn't scale. Somehow we need to find a way to delete some of it... or at the very least not backup it up AGAIN!

Size doesn't matter...

It matters not the size of your organization… today we are all dependent on IT applications used by everyone from our employees (or employee) and customers to suppliers and partners. There are a plethora of applications that support key business processes such as e-commerce, business intelligence or business communications, and it is these application that create this mountain of information that must be successfully harnessed, securely stored and continually accessible. Any organizations that don't protect this data are being pretty casual with their intellectual property

User and operator errors still account for more than 32% of permanent data loss and although server and storage hardware continue to improve efficiency and reliability, IT infrastructures are growing more complex, adding new potential points of failure.

You really need appropriate information available all the time and as we can't tell what is appropriate yet that means all of it. Non-stop, 24-hour operations need solutions that work for everything, desktops, PDAs, servers, storage... for any operating system on any hardware and any application.

Sounds like a tall order. And it doesn't matter what size you are this is still appropriate to you. Some observers estimate the growth rate of corporate data to be upwards of 60% per year. In a recent meeting with a midsized organization of around 650 employees their estimate for data growth was a manageable 20%… or so they said. In reality they were managing the growth of their structured data and completely ignoring their unstructured data growth.

Unstructured data... the curse of the modern enterprise

The thing about unstructured data is *"it's so BIG!"* you can get 25 million structured records onto 2 CDs (as HMRC demonstrated a few years back), but you can only get 25 songs onto the same space (or if you are a Progressive Rock fan two and a half Yes songs) – that's the difference between structured and unstructured data. Even semi-structured data such as from Microsoft Exchange or Lotus Domino eats up the bytes, just imagine how many documents and presentations travel through email?!?!

We now have more electronic stuff than a thing that's got a PhD in having lots of stuff[1] – where will we put it all? An estimated 988 billion gigabytes (988 quintillion bytes) of information at the last count –analysts seem to be simply making numbers up now! (Surveys have shown that accurate numbers are no more constructive than ones that have been "made up".) In reality no one really has a handle on the amount of data we create, save again,

[1] For all Blackadder fans

copy, replicate, save again, mirror, or save again and then backup up … over and over again. John Thompson, Symantec's ex-CEO stated recently that if a grain of sand represented a byte of data then we are about to exceed the grains of sand on all the beaches in the world – makes you think, doesn't it?

So we've all gone digital and we're creating a bunch of stuff and it's really important and we have to make sure we don't lose it, blah, blah, blah!

Yeah, yeah, heard it all before.

Ah, but this time connectivity is not the problem – where are the new data centers being built? Near the users… nope, near the power. And that's because power degrades the further you are away from it whilst 3rd generation fibre optics can now push 1 trillion bits down a single strand of fibre – that's 150 million simultaneous phone calls per second. The latency problems of a few years ago have now all but disappeared.

No, connectivity is no longer the problem – data is! And we have so many ways to create it: mainframes, UNIX systems, desktops, laptops, tablets, PDAs, smart phones, picture phones, iPods – the list goes on and on.

We have to get smart about data management and protection techniques. Using traditional methods such as backing up using full weekly or daily incremental, backup techniques, just don't work anymore.

The next generation of data protection solutions are designed for companies in the 21st century, ones that need to work 24x7. Solutions that enable us to see and manage all backup and recovery operations from a single place, regardless of geographic location. Solutions for environments that span across multiple platforms, databases, applications, devices, and architectures.

Why Backup Isn't Quite As Straightforward As It Seems

You just need a bigger pipe…

Susanna Sherrill (IT maven, 1969 -)

IF only it was as easy as it should be. Data on a computer, copy it elsewhere, i.e. back it up – job done. Whatever you look at, over time, it will become more complicated. So whether you are looking at a toaster or a TV remote control you will see that new features arrive which *"you just can't do without"* and before you know it you need a manual – just to operate a toaster! Well, the world of backup is no different, one machine and a 12 hour backup window (the time you can leave the machine alone to be backed up), and it can be simple.

Of course it's not that simple, we live in an online society and computers need to run 24 hours a day. We not only need access to information at all times, we create it at all times and on multiple devices. This chapter aims to look at some of the complications you need to consider when looking to implement a backup solution.

Increasing data

If there is one problem you need to get to grips with and not just for backup, but for IT in general, it is how much data you have in your organization and how fast it's growing.

The *how fast* question is a tough one; is this how much data you have, or how much unique data you have? Let's take a simple example for unique data, you have a laptop and you create a presentation… good so far… now you email it to five colleagues. There is now one copy on your machine and one in your sent items mailbox and another in the email system (it might be more, but let's pretend you have a sensible email system which only keeps one copy). Perhaps three of your colleagues saved the file on their laptops – we're up to six copies now… and maybe two of them copied it to a server for *safekeeping*. That's eight copies – and we haven't started yet. What if the server has mirrored storage, there's another two copies… perhaps it's replicated to mirrored storage as well… another four… So before you know it the 2MB presentation is now taking up nearly 30MB of space!

We have a habit of not throwing anything away, or deleting it in computer parlance, just in case we need it again, so over time our individual data storage requirements increase. Couple this with the increase in data that is coming into an organization and being stored or created and analyzed and stored then you begin to get the picture.

We are facing a tsunami of data, coming out of nowhere, flooding the organization and threatening to overwhelm it – and now you want to back it up!

Understanding your data and how much it's increasing is very important when looking at creating a backup solution.

> **Data vs. Information**
>
> Backup systems deal in data – to them all bits and bytes look and mean the same. While the backup solution can do some smart things with the data, such as de-duplication, it can't actually process it,
>
> It is the business application that can turn the data into useful information. Without the data, the application is useless and while you can readily get a copy of the application, the data is unique to you.

Server sprawl

So the data's a problem but there is another side – servers, or systems – computers in general. When you're small you tend to know how many systems you have and where they are, but it doesn't take long to lose control. New systems arrive on a frequent basis and are installed and up and running with the latest and greatest applications on it

The other side of this is that systems are decommissioned and disappear – not quite as quickly as the new ones arrive (remember we don't like to throw anything away) but they do go eventually. When looking at backups this missing system will cause the backup to fail(!) unless it has been removed from the backup schedule. Why? Well, the backup application will have correctly reported that it failed to backup the system in question… it only does what it's told to!

While we are talking about servers here, we should also mention desktops and laptops as well… we'll mention some of the other things later, but if servers arrive on a frequent basis, then laptops and desktops will arrive far more frequently. These too need to be considered when looking at backing data up.

It's a small world

Business people travel. Fact. Whether it is from London to Reading or from Tokyo to New York the fact is they travel and on their journeys they take a bewildering assortment of IT. Laptops, mobile phones, PDA's to name a few – and they want to use them, wherever they are. In the office, in airports, in café's and even at home, the list doesn't end there, as new ways to create and manipulate data appear on a regular basis and with the assumption that you wouldn't bother creating the information if it wasn't useful, it therefore needs to be backed up.

So, if you are in New York and it's 4pm and you need something from a system in London (where it's 9pm) then you expect to be able to get access to it. Technology is great isn't it… bandwidth is such that you can run the report on the application and get the results streamed across to you – all in the blink of an eye. Hurray.

However, traditional backup solutions require the application to be shut down and tend to use all available network for the backup to occur as quickly as possible, hence backups used to be done after everyone went home. Not so good for the person trying to work in New York.

The ever on application

We live 24x7 and therefore so do our applications. Applications don't shut-down and so the backup solution needs to take this into account. The art of backing up an application while it is still running is called a 'hot backup' and it's tough because you need to ensure that the data doesn't become corrupted or inconsistent at any time. Most *big* applications enable hot backup to happen. Just before a backup is started, the application is informed that one is going to occur – it can then get itself in a consistent state and the backup can occur. Often changes to the data are cached (or logged) while the backup is happening, so when the backup has finished the application can then reapply the changes and continue on its merry way.

From a backup perspective, the key is that the backup solution needs to be able to integrate with the applications you are using.

My application is too big

It won't be the application[2] that is too big for a backup, it is the data! We live in a world where a terabyte disk is something you have at home and so systems at work are seen as being much larger. In reality, a terabyte database is still a big application and not all that common, however you can still have an application that is too big to backup, or rather it's too big to backup using traditional methods within a suitable time frame.

Modern backup applications understand the complexities of applications with big data sets and have developed various methods of dealing with them. For example, the *block-level incremental* backup is one where only the blocks that have changed on disk since the last backup are backed up. In the case of enormous databases this

---

[2] By application here we mean business application. Financial systems running on databases, email, CAD, internal data processing applications etc. – rather than the Operating System or infrastructure solutions, such as backup.

is often less than 5% of the data file. In the case of having millions of small files (for example with telephone call records) you can use Flash Backup, which often cuts the time to backup the files by 60%. (Small files are a nuisance to backup applications as they spend all their time finding the files on the disk, rather than copying the data in the backup… the more files the worse this becomes. Flash backup solves this problem by grabbing the whole disk and then reassembling the files if required.)

Backup has been around for a while and so have the applications – fortunately backup has moved with the times and there are solutions to any problems you may have Of course, the top-of-the-range solution may be too costly for the average small/medium business, but with backup there are always cheaper options, which for most businesses are perfectly adequate!

Moving media

If you have backup tapes then you will want to store them, but you will also want to check the data on them every so often and perhaps copy the data from one tape to another (tape duplication), you may even want to consolidate the data on the tape or just move from one type of tape to another. All of these things will probably need to happen at some point – and that might be sooner than you think.

By way of an analogy… how much data do you now have on 3 ½" floppy disks? Probably none (and if you do, do you still have a working drive?), but they were common place fifteen years ago. One CD ROM (650MB) is equivalent to about 450 floppies, one DVD (4.7GB) to around 3000 floppies… One 16GB memory stick is the same

Talking zeros

We bandy about megabytes and terabytes all too often – but here's a quick guide.

1 bit = Binary digit (0 or 1)

8 bits = 1 byte

1 byte = 1 character

1024 bytes = 1 kilobyte (Kb)

1024 Kb = 1 megabyte (MB)

1024 MB = 1 gigabyte (GB)

1024 GB = 1 Terabyte (TB)

1024 TB = 1 Petabyte (PB)

1024 PB = 1 Exabyte (EB)

1024 EB = 1 Zetabyte (ZB)

1024 ZB = 1 Yottabyte (YB)

1000 is often used rather than 1024 for convenience, especially when it comes to storage.

as 11,377 floppies… one 160GB iPod to 113,777 floppies! So… here's the question which is easier to store one iPod or a whole room of floppies! As for the costs, well they are forever decreasing but suffice to say that after a period of time it is cheaper and better to move data onto newer media.

Increasing tape density

It might seem strange to continue to talk about tape when we talk about backup. The truth is that it is still a very valid medium even in the 21st Century. Tapes can be stored for a long period of time without data degradation[3], they have very few moving parts that can go wrong, they are relatively cheap and they are easily transportable. As with all electronic media their capacity continues to increase over time. The latest developments by IBM have seen densities of nearly 30GBits per square inch achieved. This will result in a single tape being able to hold 35TB of data – which is about 700 Blu-Ray disks.

PS They are not giving up… the increase in video gives rise to a massive increase in the amount of data to be backed up, so the engineers at IBM are already looking to 100Gbits per square inch.

Keeping data forever?

Do you really keep your data forever? It tends to be the safe bet, until you start to look at the costs; if you used a tape for backup everyday then you would need 365 for the year. If you had a backup strategy which rotates tapes every day for the working week and keeps one a week and then one for each month, you would only need 12+4+5, i.e. 21 tapes. Given a tape can cost between £10 and £50 each (depending on capacity and performance), the cost savings can be significant. Most tapes have a capacity of a few tens or hundreds of GB. Backup solutions keep track of tapes and the data on them, ensuring rotations and even telling you when to throw them away as they are wearing out.

[3] Putting a tape in a climate controlled archive will enable it to last for 15-30 years! At which point, the more likely problem is that you won't have any hardware to read the tape or the data. Moreover, the more you use a tape, the shorter it's lifetime – if you write to it once a day, then it will only last 9-12 months.

Increasing disk size

But disk has got so much cheaper… why are we talking tape when disk is so cheap? Good question. The price of disks has fallen off a cliff in recent years, who could have imagined that you could pop into the local computer shop and pick up a terabyte disk drive for less than £100! Back in the eighties the first *real* personal computers with a hard drive arrived on the market, they had a massive 20MB of storage and people wondered if they would ever fill it up… today's disks are 50,000 times bigger and running out of space is an issue! (Of course, back then when you wrote a letter it took up a few Kb, today it is several hundred Kb and if you add a few graphics then we are talking MBs!)

This change in disk capacity opened up a whole new world to backup – why use tape when you could use disk. Disk is quicker to restore information from, lots of people can access it at the same time and it can be easily updated and overwritten. Looks like a great solution?

It is. Modern backup solutions have the option to backup to disk and then, after a period of time to copy data to a tape as well. There are lots of benefits. Firstly, the backups are quicker as writing to disk is faster than writing to tape. Secondly, the backups can be online and so users can readily ask for their data back without the need to involve tapes, tape libraries and IT people to recover a file that they lost. In the ideal world, the recovery of data will be from disk rather than tape.

In the real world, there will always be data required from longer ago than the disk backup system can provide, so having longer term copies on tape is invaluable.

SAN, iSCSI, NDMP acronyms galore

The options for different types of storage are quite bewildering. You may have a Storage Area Network (SAN), or perhaps a Network Data Management Protocol (NDMP) device, or maybe you are running Fiber Channel over Ethernet (FCoE) in any case you will need a backup solution that can cope with what you have, so all servers and storage can be backed up.

Why replication just won't cut it

So much technology, so little time – and you need to be cost conscious. One customer that we went to see was looking at protecting their information, specifically IT business continuity in the event of a *disaster*. In their case, the number of power outages was becoming an issue (in the UK you might think about rising flood waters!) and so they needed to protect their systems. They had very little in the way of data protection so everything was possible. In the end they decided that data replication would be their best bet as they would then have a copy of the data and be able to move over to the copy in a second location if the first location went offline. They had thought they didn't need backup per se.

> Replication comes in a number of different varieties. Synchronous – it happens at the same time. Good for short distances. Asynchronous – it happens as quickly as possible, but it doesn't have to happen in all places before the application can continue. Good for long distances. Batch – happens on a periodic basis. Good in various circumstances where bandwidth is an issue.

Data corruption is a disaster although it is often not thought about and replicated data won't help. When a system or application fails, it is fairly obvious, the application has stopped, you can't contact the machine – there is a real problem. With data corruption the issues are not so transparent and it is even worse when the corruption is done accidently or maliciously. Imagine there is a simple upgrade which changes a few fields in a database or deletes a few files – you probably don't have to imagine that hard as this happens all the time! In a replicated environment these changes also occur on the secondary side as well – it wouldn't be much of a replication system if the two copies are not kept synchronized. Now if there is a problem, and this might not become apparent until a little while later, where will you find the copy? The secondary replicated version is as bad as the primary one. Tape backups provide you with a history of the data so you can keep looking back through them until you find an uncorrupted version – restore that one and reapply the new transactions. Or you can easily restore the deleted files. (Obviously this is not a trivial task, but at least you now have a starting point.)

A simple example of malicious corruption, in case you think it couldn't happen to you. One less than happy employee decided to change all the phone numbers in a contact database – not delete them, just randomly change a single digit. There was a dawning realization that something was wrong when customers were called but the numbers were wrong. As it was individuals who had the problems, they just thought the number had changed or it had been mistyped originally it took time to put two and two together and figure out what had happened. Restoring the data from the backup and replacing the phone fields proved to be a relatively simple fix – but would have been impossible without the backup tapes.

Should I run away now?

It's very simple to look at some of the complications and decide that, actually, backup is not for you – not because you don't need it, but because we have made the prospect look rather daunting. But take heart…

When we first started developing and marketing backup products, almost 15 years ago, they were big and complex and took a while to install and configure. It was strange because (probably a bit like you), we thought it couldn't be that tough – you just copy some data from A to B and that's that. Efficiency wasn't necessarily a watchword we had. A couple of years later, an engineering VP set us a challenge – install, configure and start the first backup… in 10 minutes. There were cries of despair and shouts of impossible as there always is when you ask an engineer to do something they haven't thought about before. However, heads were put together and a plan made. Wizards, defaults, assumptions, templates were all thrown into the mix and we got the time down to 30 minutes and then down to 8 minutes… 8 minutes from when it used to take a couple of days – wow. Of course there were assumptions made which couldn't necessarily be used in a production environment, but we found that a lot of the time they could.

Backup software was getting simpler. Well, simpler to use, even if under the covers it was becoming a lot more sophisticated. So, don't give up hope yet – there is a solution out there for you… if you only knew the Smart Questions to ask.

Just As You Thought You Understood Backup

Out of intense complexities, intense simplicities emerge

Winston Churchill (British Prime Minister, 1874 – 1965)

SURELY there can't be any more complications? It would seem that there was enough complexity in something that initially appeared so simple without adding yet more?

This is true, but if you are a growing company, then you need to start looking to the future and how trends and practices might affect your decision making. If you are really looking to the future from an IT perspective, then understanding how your IT environment is changing is important when looking at backup.

Going mobile

One piece of technology that has changed greatly in the past few years is the mobile phone. Phones used to be used for calling people on (oh so 20th Century)… they now do just about everything that a laptop can do. Email is the application that has driven smart phone adoption; ten years ago it used to be the privilege of senior executives, whereas today almost everyone has it. From a backup perspective, email is simple as the incoming and outgoing mail travels through the corporate system at some point and so backup can happen there. However, smart phones are getting smarter and people are doing more and more with them – including creating unique content. It's this unique content that needs to be looked at from a backup perspective – while people may not currently type large documents, the advent of holographic keyboards and projectors in the phones mean that soon they will. Today they are used to take pictures of signed documents as a record and to edit items which need a small change before being given to a customer.

These documents don't go through email and so are not necessarily caught by the corporate network. When looking at a backup solution, understanding the changing working practices of people becomes an important issue.

Of course the other thing that happens with the mobile phone is… we lose them. In the first 6 months of 2009, 60,000 mobile devices were left behind in London taxis[4] (as well as 12 dead pheasants, 6 toilet seats, some funeral ashes, and 2 children). Multiply this up across the globe and you start to see how bit the problem of lost data is. A typical organization loses 5-10% of their laptops per year[5] which means, even this year, there's going to be over 2.5 million missing laptops… and because you are 22 times more likely to lose your mobile phone that means over 50 million phones will go missing. Makes you wonder where they'll end up, what will be lost if they aren't backed up and how long it would take to recreate the information lost?

While we are on the subject of the mobile workforce, it is also worth considering other means that employees may use to work, particularly when at home. Apple's iPad has just been launched and while it is not a laptop, it might be something that takes the place of the laptop (or more likely the netbook), or how about using a games console to access the corporate network? OK, so people don't do it today, but these are powerful computers in their own right and they connect to the Internet – so why not use them for

4 CREDANT Technologies report, September 2008.

5 Gartner Group, 2002

work? It would save on having to buy laptops for those people who don't actually need one, but for whom it would be useful to provide corporate network access?

New technology is great, but when it comes to securing corporate data you need to start looking at how the data created on it can be backed up… and if you can't back it up, then write a policy that tells people not to use that device for work. (Until such a time as an effective backup solution is available…)

Virtualized and proud of it

If there is one overused word from the past decade, it would be virtualization. Ten years ago it was talking about storage, today its talking about servers. As the technology has hardened so it has moved from the development and test environments into the production ones and with it comes a number of issues, not least is backup.

How you use server virtualization makes a difference to the backup. Let's start with the simplest way – the computer system is just the same as a normal (non-virtualized) system and so you can have a backup agent on it, and to all intents and purposes it's the same.

Alternatively, you may want to harness the power of virtualized servers and backup the whole system image – great for efficiency and for moving one virtual server from one physical machine to another or even holding a copy of it for future reference. This requires the backup application to understand a little more about virtual machines and the virtual machine image in order to back it up as a BLOB (Binary Large Object). The downside of this is that it's not too flexible when it comes to restoring the data. You can start up the entire image and extract the data, but you do need to start up the virtual machine. One of the features of the next generation of backup applications is to be able to extract data from a virtual machine image without having to start the virtual machine. So, if you suddenly decide that you need a single file, you can access that single file as easily as if it had been backed up on its own.

Fiefdoms and people

One of the most difficult barriers to overcome when putting in a backup environment, or in fact any form of IT infrastructure service is changing the culture and dealing with the people involved.

Computers and the information they contain are the lifeblood of an organization and almost everyone in an organization will depend on the systems for their day-to-day work. Announcing any form of change is always seen as bad, even if it is good! Within smaller companies there are closet IT administrators who will be the people who look after their own systems and applications as there is no-one else to do it. They will probably have their own way to back up the data – and it will work for them. For a new companywide standard for backup to be introduced, it is these people who are the key to your success.

Explaining the benefits of backup to people in the company is not hard to do; talking about resilience in the event of a disaster (even if it's a small disaster like losing a server or a lost laptop) is simple. Discussing the ability to restore lost files is great but there is a need for constant reassurance that the new solution won't damage their systems and applications and therefore their ability to work effectively.

> THE #1 GOLDEN RULE OF INTRODUCING A BACKUP SYSTEM… DON'T STUFF IT UP.

Failure is not an option... a simple mistake, like the backup not working due to an oversight or installation error, is not helpful when it comes to creating confidence that the system is a worthwhile investment. Prioritizing less important applications and those owned by people who are 100% behind the initiative can help persuade those overly protective (aka diligent) ones who believe they know what's best for their systems. New hardware introductions or upgrades are frequently used as a time to change the infrastructure, so look at introducing the backup service then for further reassurance. For the most part, showing that the new solution will save them time and effort and allow them to go back to their 'day job' will be enough to convince even the most stubborn.

The problem with success is that people want more – so when a successful backup environment is in place, people will call the help-desk more often looking for lost files and records. They will lose their common sense and look to someone other than themselves for the answer - the most common support call at the beginning tends to result in looking in the recycle bin or a different directory on the hard drive! For this reason it is important to put together some education and policies (rules) for everyone at the outset. It might be a simple email on the benefits of backup and what can and cannot be done and what will and won't be done and some timeframes associated with responding. Requests to restore accidently deleted pictures of the cat or downloaded MP3s will not be entertained! A disk based backup system will enable this type of request can be accepted – as it is the user that does the work… rather than the administrator who would have to find the right tape, put it in a drive, fire up the restore application and so on.

Not all backups are created equal

In the same vein that not all data is equally important to the organization, it should also not be assumed that the backup of that data should be the same across the board.

Identification of the most important data can help create a cost effective and efficient system. For example, the Intranet website might only be worth backing up once a week, whereas the customer database might be done twice a day.

Categorizing servers, applications and data into a limited number of categories, for example three (gold, silver and bronze), will enable a number of backup services to be defined. This will make it easier when new applications and servers are added to include them into the backup environment. Policies can then be set up in the backup application to reflect your requirements. A *gold* level of backup might have multiple backups during the day, while a *bronze* level may just have one a week.

The nightmare of bare metal

I've lost my laptop. Not necessarily something you hear every day, but actually a pretty common occurrence. These days you need to worry about data loss issues, but the other thing is to get the person back up and running and productive as quickly as possible. A quick nip down to the local computer shop can find a laptop pretty easily but what then… unfortunately a quick restore of the files on the system won't bring back the applications, but a simple restore of an image of the laptop (everything) will often result in *the blue screen of death* due to incompatibilities in the hardware from one machine to another. This is the nightmare of bare metal… from 30,000 feet one laptop is much the same as another, from 3 feet they are like chalk and cheese.

Backup solutions now have techniques known as bare metal restore, where the backup from one system can be successfully restored onto another – lock, stock and barrel. The backup application *understands* which bits of the backup to apply and which bits to leave alone – the result is a laptop that's up and running first time.

Legislation, compliance and governance

The past few years has not only seen increases in computing power and data but also in the number of pieces of legislation governing business and the rise of compliance to prove that this is so. While there are lots of pieces of legislation that might be applicable, we are also seeing *governance* being introduced which wraps up compliance along with best practice on how a company should be run.

From a compliance standpoint, keeping appropriate data for a specific period of time is probably the most common. There are a number of ways that this can be achieved and one of the most cost effective of these is backup. In the *olden* days, let's say about five years ago (!) the most common way to achieve an archive was using a backup. The backup would be tagged as an archive copy and the data kept for the minimum required period, say seven years. If there was a requirement to recover the information, then a copy was at-hand in the backup.

So, while backup can save your business in the event of a disaster, it can also help out when the auditor comes to visit.

Data, data everywhere... Now what did I call it?

Even if your organization is small, then the quantity of data it produces can be mind boggling. Email, document files, data base reports, presentations; over the course of a year a lot of information is created. Finding it can be a problem! Backups may well have a copy of the information you need but traditionally you needed to know the name of the file before you could search for it. These days, the next generation of backup solutions is introducing full-content indexing. This is where all the information in the files is indexed so that you can search on that, rather than just the name of the file. Couple this with disk based backup (so the users can restore the data themselves) and all of a sudden the backup environment becomes a significant piece of the corporate memory – and therefore useful on a daily basis.

The problems of MP3s

Have you got any copyrighted music on your computer? It's a simple question – and the chances are that you do. Nothing wrong with that… but when it comes to backup it can cause an issue. You, as the owner of the music can have a copy on your machine, as it is for your own use – all good so far, but when a backup happens, at this point *the company* has a copy and while they won't (necessarily) listen to it, they are not allowed to have it – as that's piracy!

Out of the frying pan and into the fire we hear you cry. Well, there are two ways around this; the first (and most probably the easiest) is to have a company policy which prevents people from putting their own music on company systems. This relies on people doing the right thing but is now a common practice. The second is for the backup system to ignore MP3s or other specific types of file. This too is relatively easy to set up, although with the use of podcasts and video becoming commonplace in the corporate world this is much more difficult as not backing up these files could result in not backing up essential corporate information.

Technology is available to look inside files like MP3s and look at meta data for specific tags – if the tags are there then the file is allowed on the system, if not then the file is deleted (or just not stored in the first place.) This can then be used in conjunction with the backup system so that it knows to backup all files – as they are then known to be safe.

Travels with my backup

By now you should have realized that backup can be pretty complicated. Even in the simplest case, the backup should not be kept near the original and this can cause additional problems. If you are on a big site, then having the backups stored in one building that is separate from the data center is not a bad solution (providing the whole site isn't liable to flooding… or power outages…) but that is not often a solution for the smaller business. Often the solution is to take the backup with you. Perhaps it's a tape or two, or maybe a removable disk. This is fine but you need to do two things; firstly keep track of what is where and secondly look at encryption.

Fifteen years ago when we first discovered backup, it was often said that the easiest way to steal corporate secrets was to steal the backup tapes. This made good sense as all the important data a company had, from multiple machines, was all stored on a handy tape which you could pop into your backpack and read at leisure later. These days, data leaks and loss of confidential information makes the pages on a regular basis, so if you have a backup which goes offsite then it should be encrypted – especially if it contains customer data.

Once you start to encrypt backups, then a whole new set of problems can occur with managing the encryption keys. If you were to lose the key, then you would lose access to the data on the backup – and it would be just as useful as if you didn't back the data up in the first place!

Backup applications today manage offsite backups, letting you know what you have where and also manage encryption keys, thereby removing the issues that can occur.

Across The Internet

Just as you thought you knew all the potential complications that could occur with backup along comes the Internet to create yet more confusion. Data is increasing but so is bandwidth – giving us the ability to move vast quantities of data from one piece of cyber-space to another in a reasonable timeframe. This is good news as one of the key pieces of a backup is that it is far enough away from the original data source to be safe in the event of a disaster, while it is close enough to be able to be used quickly and easily.

You can use the Internet for backup in a number of different ways. The first is to augment an existing backup solution whereby data is moved to Internet storage as part of the process. In general, the backup data is stored locally, but some gets migrated or copied to the Internet service provider. This has the benefit that you have a copy locally should you need it, and there is a copy held (hopefully) safely by someone else.

There are a few issues that you need to think about when looking to use an Internet based backup provider and you will find these towards the end of this book.

Moving Forwards

Information is the heart of our companies today – and the increase in information is putting a strain on existing IT infrastructures. We need backup, not just as an insurance policy for something going wrong, but also for increasing compliance and legislative reasons. Many companies now operate 24 hours a day, seven days a week, 365 days a year, so traditional backup solutions (including the *it won't happen to me* option) are not up to supporting the new ways of working. We need to get smart and look at the latest technologies to help find the right solution for the company today as well as one that will take us into tomorrow.

Time to throw down the gauntlet and start asking the Smart Questions…

Ask the Smart Questions

If I have seen further it is by standing on the shoulders of giants

Isaac Newton (Scientist, 1643 – 1727)

SMART Questions is about giving you valuable insights or "the Smarts". Normally these are only gained through years of painful and costly experience. Whether you already have a general understanding of the subject and need to take it to the next level or are starting from scratch, you need to make sure you ask the Smart Questions. We aim to short circuit that learning process, by providing the expertise of the 'giants' that Isaac Newton referred to.

Not all the questions will necessarily be new or staggeringly insightful. The value you get from the information will clearly vary. It depends on your job role and previous experience. We call this the 3Rs.

The 3 Rs

Some of the questions will be in areas where you know all the answers so they will be **Reinforced** in your mind.

You may have forgotten certain areas so the book will **Remind** you.

And other questions may be things you've never considered and will be **Revealed** to you.

How do you use Smart Questions?

The structure of the questions is set out in Chapter 5, and the questions are in Chapters 6 and 7. The questions are laid out in a series of structured and ordered tables with the questions in one column and the explanation of why it matters alongside. We've also provided a checkbox so that you can mark which questions are relevant to your particular situation.

A quick scan down the first column in the list of questions should give you a general feel of where you are for each question vs. the 3Rs.

At the highest level they are a sanity check or checklist of areas to consider. You can take them with you to meetings or use as the basis of your ITT. Just one question may save you a whole heap of cash or heartache.

In Chapter 8 we've tried to bring some of the questions to life with some real-life examples.

We trust that you will find real insights. There may be some 'aha' moments. Hopefully not too many sickening, 'head in the hands – what have we done' moments, where you've realized that your company is hopelessly exposed. If you are in that situation, then the questions may help you negotiate yourself back into control.

In this context, probably the most critical role of the questions is that they reveal risks that you hadn't considered. On the flip side they should also open up your thinking to opportunities that you hadn't necessarily considered. Balancing the opportunities and the risks, and then agreeing what is realistically achievable is the key to formulating strategy.

The questions could be used in your internal operational meetings to inform or at least prompt the debate. Alternatively they could shape the discussion you have with backup application vendors, value added resellers or Internet backup service providers.

How to dig deeper

Need more information? Not convinced by the examples, or want ones that are more relevant to you specific situation? The Smart Questions micro-site for the book has a list of other supporting material. As this subject is moving quickly many of the links are to websites or blogs.

And of course there is a community of people who've read the book and are all at different levels of maturity who have been brought together on the Smart Questions micro-site for the book.

And finally

Please remember that these questions are NOT intended to be a prescriptive list that must be followed slavishly from beginning to end. It is also inevitable that the list of questions is not exhaustive and we are confident that with the help of the community the list of Smart Questions will grow.

If you want to rephrase a question to improve its context or have identified a question we've missed, then let us know to add to the collective knowledge.

We also understand that not all of the questions will apply to all businesses. However we encourage you to read them all as there may be a nugget of truth that can be adapted to your circumstances.

Above all we do hope that it provides a guide or a pointer to the areas that may be valuable to you and helps with the "3 Rs".

Backup Questions

For every complex problem, there is a solution that is simple, neat and wrong.

H.L. Mencken (Journalist & Satirist, 1880-1956)

NOW we are ready to get down to business. There are a lot of questions you can ask around backup! The next two chapters are designed to get you up to speed on backup terms and methods and then to help you find the right solution for your organization.

Chapter 6: Talking about backup

These first sets of questions will help you make up your mind as to whether you need backup and what it is you need backed up. They will also help you understand some of the terminology that's out there.

The six sections in Chapter 6 cover the following topics:

1. Before you begin, do you need backup – do you need to justify needing backup? Here are some quick questions to ask to focus the mind… even if you have backup already.
2. Are you ready for backup? High level questions to ask internally, before you start.
3. Questions to ask about your IT environment before you begin looking for a solution.
4. Backup technology basics. Get to grips with some of the terminology before you start to talk to suppliers
5. Questions about storage media and the effects on other parts of the IT environment.

6. Yet more questions which are aimed at growing knowledge around backup.

Chapter 7: Finding the right solution

Once you have decided to implement or update your backup solution you then need to find the right supplier. These sets of questions will help you find the right product or service you need.

1. Questions for your potential supplier.
2. Further questions on how they would approach the problem of providing you with a solution.
3. Questions for a potential Internet backup service provider.

Talking About Backup

Leadership and learning are indispensable to each other.

John F Kennedy (former US President, 1917-1963)

IMPLEMENTING any form of IT solution is not a decision that is taken lightly. Before you begin you need to develop the business case and get buy-in from the other people within your organization. You then need to understand what it is you are looking for with respect to your IT environment – which means you need to understand your IT environment, servers, applications, storage and all.

Finally, just as your IT environment is complex, so too are options for backup. If there was "one solution fits all" it would make life easier, but it's not like that, so you will need to understand some of the backup technology fundamentals – and some of the more complex ideas as well.

6.1 Questions for the CIO

OK, so you may not have a CIO, it may be the IT director or someone else who is responsible for IT – when it comes down to it, it may just be you. In essence if you answer yes to one or more of these questions, then a backup solution should be towards the top of your to-do list.

If you already have a backup solution, and you answer yes to some of the questions, then it is time to revisit what you have and make some changes.

☒	Question	Why this matters
☐	6.1.1 Have you ever lost data?	This is perhaps the most obvious question to ask if you are considering a backup system. That loss may be from a crashed computer or perhaps an accidental delete or maybe you know it is on the system but you just can't find it! If you have, and that loss has cost you time (and therefore money) then a backup system should be considered.
☐	6.1.2 Worried that you don't have a copy of critical data?	If you lie awake at night worried that if a computer crashes then you will lose critical business information (customer databases, orders, product designs, …) then you should think about a backup system – which will put your mind at rest and let you sleep easier at night!
☐	6.1.3 Are you concerned that someone may leave the company with some information you need?	Have you ever had someone leave the company and then you find you don't have a copy of the important information they held? If so, then having a backup application will mean that you will have a copy of the information you need. It should be noted that the person might not have left, they may have had their laptop stolen, or perhaps they are struck down with an illness and can't help you find the information you are after! Or they may just have gone on holiday… when you suddenly need some information from their laptop.
☐	6.1.4 Nervous that you might not have information you need for compliance reasons?	If you need to retain information for compliance reasons, then a backup system may be all you need. CD ROMs or DVDs can be used as an immutable (unchangeable) backup media – suitable for compliance. When the data has expired then a suitable media destruction mechanism needs to be considered.

☒	Question	Why this matters
☐	6.1.5 Are you confident you can get back company data quickly enough in the event of a disaster?	Disasters are an obvious problem which backup can help to resolve. The other area is compliance where a request could come in requiring access to data from some time ago. The backup application can be used to find and restore copies of data that can subsequently be used to satisfy the request.
☐	6.1.6 How do you define a disaster?	The obvious one is that the building is destroyed – but in all probability it's pretty unlikely. Far more likely is that you might be flooded – and it may take time to sort it out. The next level of disasters are things like power cuts – which can take out systems, but may come back in minutes or hours. Or perhaps mis-configured updates which take out several machines in one go. They don't occur all that often, perhaps once or twice a year. The third level of disaster is a system that breaks, or a laptop that is lost. These happen all the time, and if you are a larger organization, it really is *all the time* as I'm sure you know only too well. Backup is there whether you have lost a building or a laptop. A quick risk analysis will uncover the events you are trying to cover for.
☐	6.1.7 Anxious that IT is not adequately covered in your business continuity plan?	Business continuity (BC) plans, especially for smaller companies, tend to be non-existent or overlook IT. As almost all companies now depend on IT, this should be nearer the top of the BC list. Backup is a quick, effective and cheap solution for your IT environment (but remember you will need to have contingency plans for the hardware to run the applications on!)

☒	Question	Why this matters
☐	6.1.8 Do you back up all your data or just some of it?	Backing up just the data on your servers is not 'all' your data. You might have a policy which requests that laptop users copy their data onto a central server for backup – but the chances are they don't! Backup solutions should be all encompassing, and in order to be effective should be as transparent to the user as possible.
☐	6.1.9 Uneasy as to whether the right data is being backed up?	Your IT environment is probably quite complex and one concern is that not all the right data is being backed up. Coverage tools are available to ensure that all the servers and applications are adequately being backed up.
☐	6.1.10 Afraid that your virtual machines are not being backed up?	Virtualization has moved out from the dev/test environment into production environments and typically less than a third of virtual machines (VMs) are adequately backed up. Critical data is now being held on these VMs, so a backup strategy needs to take them into account.
☐	6.1.11 Are you fretful that the backup will fail?	Good reporting tools in the backup application will help ensure that if a backup does fail, you will be able to locate and resolve the problem quickly and efficiently.
☐	6.1.12 When was the last Disaster Recovery rehearsal carried out?	Once the concerns over failing backups have receded, the next concern is that you won't be able to restore your data. Disaster recovery practices coupled with periodic data checks will put your mind to rest over the quality of the data you are backing up.
☐	6.1.13 Anxious that your backup process means that your apps / email is down for too long?	Old style backup meant that applications had to be shut down while the backup took place. Newer solutions enable the application to continue to run while the backup occurs.

☒	Question	Why this matters
☐	6.1.14 Nervous that your backup tapes might fall into the wrong hands?	If not, then you should be – after all they contain all the most important information in your company. A data leak is often headline news and can be catastrophic for a company! For media on-site it should be physically secure, for media going offsite – it should be encrypted and then held in a physically secure manner.
☐	6.1.15 Are you confident that your backup tapes won't wear out?	If you are new to backup, then you probably won't have realized that backup tapes do wear out! A worn out tape will be a problem as the data integrity will be compromised. Backup applications manage tape aging and will migrate data to newer tapes if required.
☐	6.1.16 Thinking that your backup costs are too high?	Multiple backup systems or old out-of-date backup media can both lead to higher than necessary backup costs. Revisiting the backup infrastructure every 2-3 years will minimize costs. Often buying licenses on an as-needed basis versus a site-license will reduce costs and vendors will help in assessing the number of licenses you need. If you use an online backup service, then pay-as-you-go can help ensure minimizing costs. Watch for price breaks on number of users / systems backed up as well as quantity of data backed up.
☐	6.1.17 Do I really need a backup?	If you don't think you do, then read no further – but it might be worth thinking about it, especially if you rely on a computer on a daily basis!

6.2 High Level Internal Questions

Is your company ready for a backup solution to be deployed? Before you begin, it's worth thinking through some of the risks and consequences.

Cost and responsibility always raise their ugly heads, so there are a few questions to help you get the ball rolling.

☒	Question	Why this matters
☐	6.2.1 Why do I really need a backup?	Computers go wrong. If you haven't had a computer fail and lost some important information (and cursed and sworn at the screen) then it's only a matter of time before you do. Even if you haven't, then you have probably heard of friends, or read about stories in the news. Bottom line – if you rely on one or more computers for your business, then you should have a backup solution. So think about why and where you use computers, email, web site, accounts, etc.
☐	6.2.2 What types of problem can having a backup help?	In essence, backup is an insurance policy – in the event of an IT disaster, backup is there to recover your data and get you back to doing what you do best. Making money. IT disasters come in all shapes and sizes, from the loss of a building (fire, flood, power outage), the loss of a laptop – which can be just as disastrous, especially if it's your laptop, all the way down to the loss of an important file.
☐	6.2.3 Isn't tape dead?	*But backup uses tapes doesn't it and tape is really old technology!* Well, tape still has a lot going for it, it's cheap, portable, easily stored… So, while tape might not be top of your list, investing in a solution which can use tape is a good idea.
☐	6.2.4 Isn't it all about restore?	This one of the key points about backup – it's all about getting data back, restoring the information when you need it. There can be a lot of technology involved which makes backup easy, but if the restore doesn't work, then you might as well never have bothered in the first place.

☒	Question	Why this matters
☐	6.2.5 How much does a backup cost?	How long is a piece of string? Backup when it comes down to it is a continuum and so it really depends on all sorts of factors – how much data do you have, how long do you want to keep backup copies and so on. Which technology do you want to use and who will run the service – internal or external? Once you have figured out what it is you want to do and then you can figure out what the costs are likely to be. While you are thinking about costs – the other interesting one is to look at how much you would lose per hour or day should the system (or systems) fail and you had to start from scratch. Now where was that address book again..?
☐	6.2.6 Who pays for backup in an organization?	Traditionally it has been something that 'IT' has paid for in its budget – after all it is a service that they provide. That having been said, there are now better ways to monitor usage and so a more granular billing is possible. By dividing up the overall cost, it is possible to see where savings can be made – and there is nothing like a bill to focus the mind of the users!
☐	6.2.7 Are there different ways to backup information?	The million dollar question. Yes – and that's part of the problem. If there was just one way to do things, then making a recommendation for a solution would be easy, but because there are a multitude of different methods for backup you need to match the method to the data to your needs.

☒	**Question**	**Why this matters**
☐	6.2.8 Who is responsible for backup?	This is an important question. If you don't have a formal backup policy, then you will probably find that there are different backup solutions already in place inside your organization – from individuals who copy their laptop onto a USB drive to departments who have attached a tape drive (or big USB drive) to their departmental server. Discovering all the different mechanisms and people who currently do backup means that you can enlist them to help create the new companywide service. Ultimately, backup is the responsibility of the person who looks after IT, whether that is a CIO, IT Director or 'Bob from sales' who is IT savvy and looks after the systems. Formalizing who is responsible for backup will make life simpler in the end and will save a lot of finger-pointing in the event of a disaster… *"But I thought he was responsible…"*
☐	6.2.9 Should we have a backup policy?	Yes. A backup policy simply helps to define the service. It usually has a number of components, including ones relating to what people should and shouldn't do. Copying files from desktops (and laptops) to a particular server for backup is a perfectly valid part of a backup policy – but anything that relies on people remembering stuff usually fails – so I wouldn't recommend that as a policy! However, it might tell users when backups will happen and highlight backup frequency and process / procedure to request a restore.

6.3 Your IT Environment

Understanding what you have in your IT environment will make it much easier to select the right backup solution for your company. How much data, what applications and discovering where your data is, are all part of the discovery process.

Once you have asked the questions once, then find someone else to ask them to a second time – the answers will be different and you will end up with a more complete picture. After this, it is a law of diminishing returns, so you could ask more people, but the additional information gained may not be worth the effort.

☒	Question	Why this matters
☐	6.3.1 What is the mix of Operating Systems in your organization?	Picking the right backup solution is not as easy as it might first appear. If you have a limited number of Operating Systems (OSs) then this can help reduce the selection of backup applications – and make the implementation easier.
☐	6.3.2 Which are your key applications?	This should be an obvious question to ask, where are the applications, who uses them, who owns them and when are they in use? Various categories should be used to classify them, such as business critical (perhaps your external web server and email), while others are less important (perhaps development systems and HR) – you can then design different backup policies for each category.
☐	6.3.3 How do you do backups today?	The answer to this question may well be "I don't know". The chances are that there will be individuals in your organization who do perform some kind of backup on their data and/or systems – even if it is just to copy it to somewhere else on the network. This is the way that all backup environments start – and having someone who understands the need for a backup is a good thing!

☒	Question	Why this matters
☐	6.3.4 What does your backup environment look like?	Do you have one? Or do you have many? Or do you not know if you have one or not? The chances are if you don't think you have one – you probably have several! People looking after computers, especially those with applications that many people use, tend to be paranoid – and so will have some form of backup in place. Even if it is only to copy the data onto a different system at night. Identifying what backup applications or procedures are in place will help define the type of backup system you will need.
☐	6.3.5 How many backup applications do you have today?	Probably more than you would imagine. Discovering where they are and who is using them will help in defining the backup solution you need and finding supporters of the initiative – as they won't have to do it themselves.
☐	6.3.6 What backup hardware do you already own?	If you have already invested in some backup infrastructure, for example a tape library, then you will want any new backup application to work with it. Compiling a list of backup assets before you select a vendor can save time later – not all backup applications support all backup media. Note: Just because you own a solitary backup tape drive from a few years ago doesn't mean it has to be a part of the new backup infrastructure. As with most things there is a trade-off… common sense should prevail!
☐	6.3.7 How fast is your data increasing?	If you don't understand how quickly your data is increasing, it becomes difficult to design a suitable backup solution - or at least one which will cope with your ever expanding company.

☒	Question	Why this matters
☐	6.3.8 Do you have any data classification system to separate important data from the rest?	Not all data is created equal, so therefore it doesn't all have to be backed up in the same way. Data classification can help lead to a more cost efficient backup system, with business critical data being backed up and protected more frequently than, say, development and test data.
☐	6.3.9 What is the utilization of your servers?	Server utilization figures are sometimes seen as the holy grail of efficiency. When looking at a backup system, especially if you are planning on using hot-backups (where the application continues to run), it is important to understand the utilization in order to figure out if backup will have a serious performance hit on the running applications.
☐	6.3.10 How often do you add a new server to the IT environment?	This is another important question – every time a new server is commissioned (or decommissioned) it needs to be added (or removed) to the backup environment. Understanding what type of servers are used, or will be used, will help define the features you need in your backup solution.

☒	Question	Why this matters
☐	6.3.11 What do we do about laptops?	Laptops are a pain, they tend to have a lot of critical data on them and yet the owners don't back them up! Many organizations have a policy (which is often ignored) of asking laptop users to copy data onto a central server – which is then backed up. As it is ignored a better solution is needed. Laptop backup solutions only backup the differences since the last backup, and in the case of large files (for example offline email archives), then only the changes in the files are backed up. As not much data changes on a laptop, this means an automated backup can occur each time a user connects to the network, so protecting the data.
☐	6.3.12 What do we do about mobile phones and PDAs?	In many cases, the data on mobile phones and PDAs is also transferred (or synchronized) with other servers which are part of the backup environment. However, as more people look to create more and more unique information on these devices, so they should be included in the backup environment with backup client agents.
☐	6.3.13 Do you have remote offices?	If you do, then is there a backup happening there? Backup across multiple sites can be centrally managed and reduce administration costs. The backup data can be pulled back to a central location (good for disaster recovery for the remote sites) or stored locally for easy access. In many cases, the backup solutions can be implemented at remote sites and then 'joined' into the main backup environment at a convenient point in the future.

☒	Question	Why this matters
☐	6.3.14 Can I use backup for disaster recovery / business continuity?	Yes. The primary purpose for backup is for use in the event of a disaster… no matter how large or small that disaster may be. It might be that someone has lost their laptop (a disaster for them!) or it might be there has been a gas explosion and the main data center has been knocked out – both can rely on their backups to get them back up and running again.
☐	6.3.15 Do you use virtual machines?	Virtual machines are now creeping into everyday use, and so need to be considered when putting together a backup strategy. The most modern of backup solutions enable virtual machines to be backed up in a number of different ways to suit your usage needs.
☐	6.3.16 Is there data you don't want backed up?	This may seem a strange question – surely all data on business systems should be backed up? Actually there are some items you don't want to backup like temporary files or perhaps MP3s. The backup solution you implement should be able to ignore (exclude) the data types you don't want or need to be backed up.
☐	6.3.17 Can I use backups for legal compliance?	Yes you can – but you need to be careful as to what is and isn't covered. For example, backing up email for compliance is only ok, if every email in and out of the system is backed up… if the system has not been set up appropriately, then an email could be sent and/or received and then deleted between backup runs, thereby removing the compliance.

☒	Question	Why this matters
☐	6.3.18 Is one copy of the data enough?	How many copies you have is a trade-off between money and flexibility (and complexity). The more copies you have, the more it will cost to keep them – on the other hand, you might keep copies at several locations in your organization so there will always be one close at hand! For smaller companies, the rule of thumb is to keep one copy per year, plus one copy for each of the past 12 months, plus one copy for the past 5 weeks plus one copy for the last 5/7 days. The idea being that this will cover all eventualities. After this, you may like to keep a duplicate copy of some or all of these.
☐	6.3.19 Would moving old data help you?	Within an organization, most of the data is old – where old can mean 30 days or two years. Old data is often infrequently accessed and so could be moved off to cheaper storage – this frees up existing storage for growth and speeds up the backups, as the old data won't need to be backed up on such a frequent basis. Archiving is where old data is copied to somewhere else and then deleted from the primary storage. Backup solutions can be enabled to do this – for example, archiving data that hasn't been accessed for 180 days.
☐	6.3.20 Would you benefit from moving to newer storage?	The answer to this question is always yes – whether you can afford to move is a different question. Undoubtedly you will have a storage replacement plan, part of which will involve migrating data. Backup applications can help in several ways, including moving old data off the system, so making the transition of current data faster.

6.4 Backup Technology Basics

This next set of questions are *the obvious* ones about backup technology. They are ones you could ask your backup application vendor, but are more likely to be ones which they might assume you already know.

Never be afraid to ask a question, no matter how simple it may be – it will help in your understanding and more importantly help the other person with how you understand the problem at hand.

☒	Question	Why this matters
☐	6.4.1 What is a backup?	A backup is an organized copy of all your important business data from across the entire IT environment.
☐	6.4.2 What is a full backup?	A full backup is a copy of ***all*** the files in the IT environment. A full backup is effectively when you copy all your data from one place to another. Because of the amount of data we are now trying to backup, full backups can become lengthy – if not impossible.
☐	6.4.3 What's the difference between a tape drive and tape library?	In essence a tape drive is the mechanical device that reads and writes tapes. These drives can be stand-alone, i.e. you have to put the tapes in yourself, or it could be in a library, which has a number of tapes which can be automatically inserted. The biggest tape libraries have multiple drives and can hold thousands of tapes! Not all tape drives / libraries are supported by all backup applications – so if you have any tape infrastructure you want to reuse, you may need to check for compatibility before you start the selection process.
☐	6.4.4 What's a backup window?	The backup window is the period of time that you have to complete a backup. In environments where everybody goes home and the systems are shut down, then this could be overnight, i.e. 12 hours. The increasing data and requirements for 24 hour working means that the backup window is shrinking, and in some cases is zero… in which case other backup technologies are needed to meet the backup requirement.

☒	Question	Why this matters
☐	6.4.5 What's RPO? (Recovery Point Objective)	There are two acronyms backup vendors will throw at you, RPO and RTO (see below). The recovery point objective is a measure of how much data you are willing to lose in a disaster. If you are happy to lose a week of data then the RPO is a week – and the choice for a backup product and policy can be reflected in this. If, on the other hand you are only willing to lose 2 seconds, then the technologies and policies are different – and more costly! Not all applications and data need the same RPO!
☐	6.4.6 What's RTO? (Recovery Time Objective)	This is the second of the acronyms used. The Recovery Time Objective (RTO) is the time taken to recover the data. If you can survive without an application for a week, then the RTO is a week and the ways and means of recovering the data will be different from something that you want back up and running in 2 minutes. The shorter the RTO, the most costly it is to implement. As with RPO, not all applications need the same RTO. Prioritizing applications and figuring out what is needed in terms of RPO/RTO will help define the backup technologies you require.
☐	6.4.7 What's a three tier backup architecture?	In essence of a three tier architecture provides a scalable solution. The three components are: 1. The master server 2. The media server 3. The client Additionally, there are now a number of solutions which add a fourth *umbrella* tier to the architecture to enable greater scalability and visibility across, what was previously separate, backup regions.

☒	Question	Why this matters
☐	6.4.8 What does the master backup server do?	This is the brains behind the backup system. In essence it knows what resources are available (tapes, drives, disks etc) and what needs to be done – backup of applications, file systems, etc. At the heart of the master server is a piece of code called the scheduler which aligns all the pieces and gets the backup to happen in a timely manner.
☐	6.4.9 What's a media server?	The media server is the system that has a backup device attached to it. For example a tape library. Data is routed from the backup clients to the media server at the request of the master server. The more data you have the more media servers you (may) need to ensure all the data gets backed up in the backup window.
☐	6.4.10 What's a backup client?	This is the system with the data on it. It could be a laptop, or a server. It could be an email system or a website or a mobile phone. The client is backed up using a backup agent – this in effect is a small application which transfers the data to the media server when requested. It enacts the policies as outlined by the master server, for example which files to ignore. In some cases the client and the media server are one-in-the-same. For example for a big database, it might be more effective for the tape library to be attached to the same server as the database.

☒	Question	Why this matters
☐	6.4.11 Is there something special for backing up applications?	Yes. There are special backup agents for applications. These understand the application and know where to find the various pieces for a backup. For example, where the data files and configuration can be found. In the case of a hot backup, then it also understands how to interact with the application to put it into a state whereby the backup can occur while the application continues to run.
☐	6.4.12 What's an incremental backup?	This is a backup of files which have changed (or been created) since the last backup. As there a less files it therefore takes less time to complete!
☐	6.4.13 What's block level backup?	Backup is traditionally done by taking a complete file and backing it up sequentially. However, files are made up of blocks – and in certain circumstances, backing up the blocks is much more efficient.
☐	6.4.14 What's BLIB?	Once you can identify which blocks on a disk have changed, then you can go one step further in backing them up – by only backing up those that have changed since the last backup hence Block Level Incremental Backup (BLIB). This technique is idea for backing up massive databases – as the vast majority of the blocks don't change, so BLIB can make for a very fast solution to what would otherwise be a very difficult problem.
☐	6.4.15 What's flash backup?	Flash backup is a mechanism for backing up a file system really quickly – using the blocks rather than the files. Files can be reconstituted if required when restored. This is a very efficient way to backup lots of small files.

☒	Question	Why this matters
☐	6.4.16 What's a hot backup?	A hot backup is specifically used to describe backing up an application while it is still running.
☐	6.4.17 What's off-host backup?	Storage can be shared between two or more computer systems. It is possible to use one of the other systems to perform the backup, rather than the one with the application on. This means that the server with the application doesn't have any processor overhead while the backup is being taken and therefore the performance of the application is unaffected.
☐	6.4.18 What's LAN free backup?	Most backups occur over the LAN, i.e. your normal network – or by a directly attached device. The advent of fibre channel and storage area networks (SANs) have created the opportunity to carry out backups which don't affect the LAN – by passing the data across the SAN.
☐	6.4.19 What's forever incremental backup?	Some data is just too huge to backup. In this case, the only option is only to backup the data which has changed – and then to recreate the complete data set offline using a synthetic backup.
☐	6.4.20 What's a synthetic full backup?	A synthetic full backup is one made up from an old full (or synthetic full) backup plus all the relevant incremental backups. This means that when a restore is needed, all the relevant files are all together – making the restore much faster.
☐	6.4.21 What's tape streaming?	Tape is sequential! (Disks allow for random access…) This means there is an optimal rate to write data to a tape – when this happens it is called streaming. The trick is for the backup application to have enough data queued up from the various backup clients to ensure that the tape streams. If the tape doesn't stream, then it keeps rewinding and fast forwarding to find the correct position for the next bit of data.

☒	**Question**	**Why this matters**
☐	6.4.22 What's multiplexing?	Multiplexing is taking data from multiple sources and putting it onto the backup media. This often occurs with smaller systems, where several computers can be backed up in parallel to a single tape drive.
☐	6.4.23 What's de-duplication?	In essence, this is where only one copy of a piece of data is backed up. For example, if you backup lots of laptops, then there are a large number of files which are the same on each – having backed up one copy, the system then makes a note of others, but doesn't request that the data be transferred. De-duplication speeds up backups and saves storage. It is most often used in laptop backup and when using disk based backup storage.
☐	6.4.24 What is block-level de-duplication?	For large files, it is possible to de-duplicate at the block level, offering greater granularity. As this can be processor intensive, it is only done for files over a certain size.
☐	6.4.25 What's the difference between single-instance-storage (SIS) and de-duplication?	SIS and de-duplication are basically the same – the outcome is a reduction in storage. However, SIS tends to be used more for files and de-duplication is increasing used to refer to block-level de-duplication.
☐	6.4.26 What's a duplicate backup image?	A duplicate backup image is just what it sounds like – it is a copy of another backup image. These copies are usually made after the first one is made – so it doesn't impact the network. The copy can then be stored offsite for disaster recovery purposes – while a local copy can be maintained for 'everyday' recovery needs.

☒	Question	Why this matters
☐	6.4.27 What's real-time or continuous backup?	For some applications the backup frequency is required to be real-time (or near real-time). The backup is taken when a specific event occurs. This might be when a file is closed, or when a write has occurred. There are a number of issues relating to the amount of space that the backup then requires – which is controlled by the backup policy.
☐	6.4.28 What's point-in-time recovery?	This is a technology which will recover a system to a specific point in time and relies on the backup having additional information in it – specifically regarding which files are not there! For a full backup it's easy, as it will be all the files. When it comes to incremental backups, then you also need to know which files have been deleted (as well as those which have been changed) – if you don't know this, then you can end up trying to restore too many files for the space available.
☐	6.4.29 What's granular restore?	Granular restore technology is used in a number of different places where the data required (it might be a single file, or one email) is tied into a larger lump of data – such as the entire email system. Traditionally all the data had to be restored before the piece wanted could be extracted, modern backup applications can read into the structure of the data enabling individual items to be restored on demand.
☐	6.4.30 What is bare-metal restore?	This is the technology that takes a raw machine and enables a complete restore to occur, from the operating system through to all the applications and data.

☒	Question	Why this matters
☐	6.4.31 What is dissimilar hardware restore?	Systems differ from each other, and in some cases this causes problems when restoring a complete system image. (Blue screen of death and all that…) Dissimilar hardware restore can dissect a backup and figure out which pieces are relevant to the system itself (hardware related) and which are not – so avoiding any clashes which would result in the machine being unable to boot.

(Writing out this first set of questions has made me realize just how tough it is to get to grips with backup. As with anything, technical or not, there is a large amount of jargon which you need to have some idea of before you start – hopefully you are now suitably armed for the next section!)

6.5 Backup media and the effects on the IT environment

Putting in a backup system affects the entire IT environment in one way or another.

Processes will have to change if the backup is to remain reliable – to ensure the backup environment remains up to date with your ever-changing IT infrastructure. There is a new kid on the block, and it will take up network bandwidth and let's not forget budget as well. Getting some idea of where these changes are will help overcome some of the doubters, or those resistant to change.

Forewarned is forearmed.

☒	Question	Why this matters
☐	6.5.1 Can I use a CD ROM or DVD to backup my data?	Yes! CDs/DVDs are great as an immutable (unchangeable) copy of the data – which can be used for historical reasons. These days, most computer systems have a large amount of data, so a CD ROM probably won't have enough capacity for most backups. Having said that, there may be some small amount of data which you decide will be useful to backup onto CD ROMs – in which case you can set up a backup policy to do that, while everything else goes to tape or some other media.
☐	6.5.2 Can I backup to disk?	Yes. New backup systems use disk as the first line of backup media. It makes backups faster and enables users to more easily do their own data restores. While disk is the primary backup medium, tape is often still used as the secondary backup media. It's still easier for long term storage, more reliable and simpler to transport.
☐	6.5.3 Why do some vendors tell me I don't need tape?	For some vendors they can't support tape devices! For others, this is a way to tell you that backup to disk is *the way to go.* If you are a small company, it may well be that you don't need tape – but before you discard the idea, think of some of the advantages, especially around keeping a low cost copy for a long period of time. The costs of tapes and tape drives have reduced considerably so a disk-to-disk-to-tape backup system will probably cover all eventualities.

☒	Question	Why this matters
☐	6.5.4 Could I backup to my iPod™?	Yes. In fact the iPod is often used by small businesses as backup media as it is small and therefore portable, while being robust and with a good capacity (up to 160GB at the time of writing). These days a 1TB USB drive now offers a great deal more storage for a fraction of the cost of an iPod and you can still easily put it in a briefcase. Remember, if you are taking data offsite, then you should consider encryption, especially if your data contains confidential information.
☐	6.5.5 What capacity does a tape have? Or a CD ROM or DVD…	CD ROM: approx. 600MB DVD: approx. 4.7GB (9.8GB for dual layer) Blu-ray: approx 50-100GB Tape: approx. 20GB – 300+GB. With 1+TB in the near future. Tape drives can also compress the data in real time to increase capacity further.
☐	6.5.6 What about holographic storage?	Holographic storage has been (and still is to some extent) the great hope on how to deal with backing up huge quantities of data. In theory holographic storage has much greater capacity than other types of media and it will last longer – in practice, other technologies, such as Blu-Ray and the latest tape technology have caught up and have the benefit of being considerably cheaper.

☒	Question	Why this matters
☐	6.5.7 What is NDMP?	The Network Data Management Protocol was created by some storage vendors to enable data to be copied between network attached storage (NAS) devices, for example a disk array, and backup devices – without having to go through the backup server itself. This makes it faster and reduces the load on the server.
☐	6.5.8 What's a VTL?	A Virtual Tape Library (VTL) is a bunch of disks that are made to look like a tape device! Why? Well, because then it can work with all the traditional backup applications – but give a lot of the advantages of disk; scalable and fast for both backup and restore. Some VTLs move the data to tape in post-processing (disk staging) which is often called disk-to-disk-to-tape (D2D2T)
☐	6.5.9 What are SAN and NAS?	Storage Area Networks (SAN) and Network Attached Storage (NAS) are different types of storage that you find in today's enterprises. (In the case of NAS, they are now creeping into the home!) Backup strategies are available for both types of storage as well as the 'regular' storage inside systems and that which is directly attached (DAS).
☐	6.5.10 What is iSCSI?	iSCSI is a storage protocol which runs across the Internet. As networks have become quicker, so more options have become available for connecting the storage – and with those options, so too has backup had to change to support these new IT environments.

☒	Question	Why this matters
☐	6.5.11 What is CDP?	Continuous Data Protection (CDP) is an advanced technique which allows data to be backed up continuously, or at very frequent intervals. As it is *continuous*, it can use large amounts of storage and so is only used in circumstances which warrant it. Because of the way it is done, it is very quick to recover from a logical data problem (for example data corruption) and roll back to a specific point in time.
☐	6.5.12 When's the best time to run a backup?	Ideally backups are run when there is little other network traffic or application activity. Traditionally this has been between about 10pm and 6am, or at the weekends (especially for full backups).
☐	6.5.13 When's the worst time to run a backup?	Conversely the worst time for a backup is when the application is being heavily used – so during the middle of the day, or when special runs are occurring, such as at the end of the month or the end of a quarter. Understanding when applications are most heavily used will make backup planning much easier.
☐	6.5.14 Are there specific times when a backup is a good thing to do?	It might be that at the end of a month or the end of a quarter there is a great deal of processing that occurs – and so a backup could / should be taken when that has happened – even if it is out of sequence for the usual backup schedule.
☐	6.5.15 What's TAR?	TAR is short for Tape Archive – and is a standard used by Open Systems for backup tapes. In theory, TAR format tapes written by one backup application can be read by another. In practice, if there are things like multiplexing used then reassembling the backup streams is too complicated to be done by hand.

☒	Question	Why this matters
☐	6.5.16 Do tapes ever wear out?	Yes they do. Unfortunately, unlike audio tapes where a little hiss can be lived with, or a bit of tape used to splice a broken tape back together, digital data is more exact, so when a tape starts to get errors due to wear it needs to be discarded and any important data on the tape copied off onto a fresh one. Most tapes can be run through a tape drive between 100 and 150 times, so if you have one that rotates through each day of the week, then it will need to be replaced every 2-3 years. Tapes left alone on a shelf have an estimated lifespan of 30 years… which is probably long enough for most things. Even so, a data migration strategy is still a good thing to have to prevent you ending up with a container load of 3 ½" disks rather than one iPod!
☐	6.5.17 How do I move data from one tape to another?	One of the additional operations that backup applications carry out is around managing the data on tapes. It can replicate tapes or consolidate backups on tapes automatically, or upon request.

☒	Question	Why this matters
☐	6.5.18 What should I do with my backup tapes? Where should they be stored?	Backup tapes need to be stored away from where they are created – or at least some of them do. That way if there is a disaster, then the tapes will (hopefully) not be in the same area and so be available for recovery. For smaller companies, fire-proof safes are a good place to store backup tapes, and if there are a couple of different buildings, then storing a copy in 'the other building' is fine – providing you are not on a flood plain! For many customers, taking the copy home is a good idea – as long as you get into the habit of bringing it back again. (Otherwise you run out of tapes / media and then the backup doesn't happen.)
☐	6.5.19 How do I dispose of backup tapes or other media?	There are a number of ways to dispose of the media – with tapes, they can be shredded (or fluffed as it is known). CD ROMs and DVDs can be shredded as can hard-disks, although they need a little more specialized equipment to do it. For some hard-drives, overwriting them with specific patterns can be perfectly adequate. (Look up Data Erasure on Wikipedia – there are a number of free utilities that can do this for you.)
☐	6.5.20 How does backup affect the network?	Backup is traditionally very network hungry. The idea is to push as much data across the network in as short a time as possible. This can happen to the detriment of anything else happening on the network.

☒	Question	Why this matters
☐	6.5.21 What is network throttling?	Network throttling is where an application is wary of how much network bandwidth it is using. In the case of a backup application, this means that it is possible to schedule backups while other systems are running – without affecting the performance of the other systems.
☐	6.5.22 What's an exclude list?	An exclude list is all the bits and pieces you really don't want to backup – this could be MP3 files or videos but also might include system files and temporary files, if you are simply backing up your data. (If you are excluding MP3s from your backups you might ask yourself why you're storing them in the first place) Exclusions can also be complete systems that are not critical or do not hold critical data. By default the backup application will backup all files – the exclude list contains the ones it can skip. Reducing the number of files to back up reduces the time the backup will take.
☐	6.5.23 Why is it important for backup to integrate with virus scanning software?	In short, you don't want to backup virus riddled files… not because they can do damage while on a backup device, but because if they are restored they can re-infect the system and potentially the network. Integration with virus scanning can be done to prevent viruses from being introduced into the backup in the first place, as well as being used to scan files when they are restored to ensure that they are not infected upon their return.

☒	Question	Why this matters
☐	6.5.24 Why is it important for backup to integrate with HSM software?	HSM (or Hierarchical Storage Management) software basically moves old files off the main storage system and onto something cheaper. If the file is required, then the HSM system retrieves it transparently for the user. If HSM is not integrated with the backup system, then when backup scans the file to back it up, the HSM system thinks it needs to retrieve the file – and chaos ensues. With integration, the backup system in effect skips the HSM'd file.
☐	6.5.25 What does tiered backup storage mean?	Tiered storage is where there are different levels of storage based on importance. Using a web server as an example, the web pages (HTML) may be more important than the image files (JPG) – so they are stored on different types of storage. More expensive for HTML, cheaper for JPG. The same goes for backup, you can have different levels of storage for backup – and different policies for backing it up. You can also use tiered backup storage over time. Recent data may be held on disk while the older data is moved off onto cheaper tape.

☒	Question	Why this matters
☐	6.5.26 How does backup differ from archiving?	In essence, a backup takes a copy of the data and leaves the original alone, while an archive removes the original (having first made a copy of it.) Things are now a little cloudier, as many 'archiving' applications leave the original copy there as well. It should also be noted that you take a backup in order to carry out a restore (in the event of a disaster), but you take an archive copy for other reasons, such as compliance. Not all items will necessarily be in an archive – whereas they will be in a backup.

6.6 Growing Your Knowledge

As you may have figured out by now, backup is not as simple as you first thought, there are lots of different techniques for making a backup happen – depending on what you need.

This next set of questions looks at some of the other basics which will help you understand what it is you need.

☒	Question	Why this matters
☐	6.6.1 What happens if a backup fails?	Usually if a backup fails, it automatically retries it. This overcomes a number of frequent errors, such as systems being unavailable due to a network glitch.
☐	6.6.2 Why do backups fail?	Firstly, backups do fail… if a machine can't be reached because the network is down, then the backup will fail. Perhaps an application should have been shutdown and wasn't – causing the backup to fail. The good news is that by running a quick check on the backup report it is possible to see what problems have occurred and whether action needs to be taken. Another reason backup fail is that the system in question has been decommissioned, or some of the storage has been removed, but the backup application hasn't been altered – so it keeps trying to back it up… and failing. So, just as backup can be part of the commissioning process, it should also be a part of the decommissioning one as well. Finally, it might be that the backup system could have run out of space… perhaps it doesn't have enough tapes, or the disks are full. So keeping an eye on capacity is important.
☐	6.6.3 Why is reporting important?	Reporting give you peace of mind – knowing that you have a successful backup to return to in the event of a disaster is a key component of the system. Likewise understanding that there is a problem with the backup is equally important. Backup reporting tends to cover all manner of items, from backup success and failure to capacity planning and even network traffic information. For user backups, it can also estimate how long the backup will take or how long until a file is restored.

☒	Question	Why this matters
☐	6.6.4 Why is centralized management important?	Centralized management not only gives you centralized reporting, it also gives consistency for backup policy and scheduling. It enables more efficient device configuration and media management, and allows for fault tolerance and load balancing across the IT environment.
☐	6.6.5 How long does a backup take?	How long is a piece of string? It all depends… how much network bandwidth, how fast is the tape / disk drive, how much data, how many servers to be backed up. The more money spent, the faster the backup! (And hopefully the faster the restore as well…)
☐	6.6.6 What happens if my backup takes too long?	This can happen for a number of reasons. Firstly, the network might not have enough bandwidth – so you could improve the network, put in a dedicated backup network or put a media device (e.g. a tape drive) closer to the source of the data. It might be that there are too many systems to be backed up sequentially, so adding in a new tape drive (or library) will enable more to be backed up in parallel. It might be that there is just too much data, in which case looking at some newer technology, such as block-level incremental backups will be able to resolve the problem.

☒	Question	Why this matters
☐	6.6.7 Is all the data backed up at the same time?	No. The backup happens when the backup happens. So if you are backing up files, then the first file might be backed up at 7pm while the last one may be at 2am the following day. For applications, mechanisms to quiesce (put into a stable state) the application are used, so that all the data is, in effect backed up at the same time, or when you use one of the other more advanced techniques such as flash backup, the data will be backed up at the same time.
☐	6.6.8 What is one-pass backup?	For some applications, two passes need to be made through the data for the backup to occur, for example with e-mailbox backup. Single-pass is a new backup method which speeds the backup without losing restore functionality. In this case, the ability to restore a single user's mailbox without having to restore the whole email system.
☐	6.6.9 What can slow down recovery from backups?	Recovery from backup can be slowed down for a number of reasons. The first is network bandwidth – trying to recover too many systems at the same time can saturate the network and slow down the recovery. The other way recovery can be slowed is if there are multiple sources for the data. For example, if the recovery takes one tape from the last full backup and ten from the subsequent incremental backups, then this slows up recovery – and is a good reason to create synthetic full backups.

☒	Question	Why this matters
☐	6.6.10 Can I recover files to other places – not just the original one?	Yes – you can recover files to a different directory or even to a different machine. These options tend to be more carefully controlled, such that it is usually only an administrator who can recover files to a different machine for security reasons.
☐	6.6.11 What happens if I restore two files of the same name?	Depends! In general, the last file restored will overwrite the pre-existing copy. There are a number of policies that can be set which changes this default behavior, for example to rename the file – or to put it into a different directory.
☐	6.6.12 What happens if there are multiple files with the same name?	When backing up files, it is not just the file name which is taken into consideration but also the machine name and the path. Additionally, this file is part of an explicit backup – so within the backup catalog there can be multiple files of the same name, some of which may be identical – the only difference being that they are part of different backups, while others may only share the same name, but have completely different contents.
☐	6.6.13 If I recover all the files for this machine, it will run out of space!	This can be a problem, the backup takes all the files and with a restore all the files from the start of the backups may well be recovered – including those you have deleted on purpose. For this reason, there is another option when doing a backup and that is to store a list of all the files that exist at the point in time the backup is taken. This is called differential backup – in this way when you restore to a point-in-time, only those files that actually existed will actually be restored.

☒	Question	Why this matters
☐	6.6.14 What is a backup retention policy?	This is the policy which eventually deletes old backups and recycles the tapes. So, you may have a policy to keep the last five days of backups. After the time is up, the tape is marked as able to be reused – so that it can be reused. With the backup application keeping track of the media, it ensures that the data is not overwritten onto a tape (or other media) which still has *current* data as defined by the policy.
☐	6.6.15 Can I use data replication rather than backup?	If backup is a copy of your data then at first glance, replication would do the same job. However, replication won't provide you with a history of your data and won't help in the event of logical corruption – as the corruption would happen to the original and then be replicated to the copy!
☐	6.6.16 Can backups be used for versioning files?	Yes. If backups are taken regularly, then there will, by default, be several copies of the same file. In some cases it might be exactly the same when the file hasn't changed between backup runs. While using backups as a type of versioning, it should not be considered the same as file system versioning, whereby every change can create a new copy, allowing the user to go back to the document at any point in time.

Finding The Right Solution

There are no solutions… there are only trade-offs.

Thomas Sowell (Economist & social commentator, 1930-)

THERE is no right or wrong backup solution, just better or worse ones for your organization. As with most IT projects, it will all come down to money in the end, the good news is that for smaller companies, the less complicated the solution, the cheaper it will be – and the easier (and cheaper) to run.

Putting a backup solution in place is a partnership, between you, your IT department and your supplier. Openness as to what you need and how your requirements might grow are essential for a successful implementation.

7.1 Questions for Your Potential Supplier

Let's start at the very beginning – so the first couple of questions will help you weed out the suppliers who can't help you. The quicker you can do this, the quicker you can get down to finding the right solution for you.

☒	Question	Why this matters
☐	7.1.1 What backup applications do you sell?	If you know what you want, then that's great – if you are not sure, then you need a vendor who can give you a number of options so that you can find the right solution for you.
☐	7.1.2 Which OSs / devices / applications do they support?	This is the first of the nitty-gritty questions. If the application they are selling doesn't match your OS requirements, then you need to find another supplier! Get this question out there early on – and remember, you are after a solution *today*, not tomorrow. Everybody always supports everything in the next release.
☐	7.1.3 Do I need different backup solutions for Windows, UNIX, Linux and Mac?	The idea behind putting in a company-wide backup solution is to reduce the administration required to keep your data safe – so, while you could use different solutions for each platform, it is better to choose one solution that covers all your platforms. If you are just running Windows, then there are more backup solutions available than if you are running a multi-platform environment. Within small businesses, the predominant plat forms are Windows, Linux and Mac and there are backup solutions tailored for just this environment.
☐	7.1.4 Can you help with install and configuration?	You may have the skills in-house, or you may need some help – if the supplier is just a box shifter, then they won't be able to help you if you need help. Being upfront about what you require from the potential supplier will make your life (and theirs) a lot simpler.

☒	Question	Why this matters
☐	7.1.5 Can I backup my email server – even if I use it 24 hours a day?	Yes. There are a number of backup options that exist to backup email systems while they are running. If your potential supplier *umms* and *ahhs* here, then they don't have enough knowledge to help you will hot application backups. Time to try another one! However… Archiving is also becoming a key part of an email environment for legal compliance reasons – and so it may be that soon the best way to back up an email environment is to use archiving, and so this may be another solution that they suggest.
☐	7.1.6 Can I backup multiple offices?	Yes! In the biggest backup environments, there can be 100s of sites all controlled by one master server. They may have local media servers, or they might transfer the backup data to a central location.
☐	7.1.7 What if I want to join different backup regions together?	This is also possible – most backup applications now allow an overarching system to be added in, a master-of-masters if you like. This leaves the separate domains to be in charge of themselves, but to enable overall visibility into the complete backup environment.
☐	7.1.8 Can I report across multiple backup domains?	Yes. This is one of the fundamental features of a master-of-masters type of application. This can also help in planning and load balancing in the future.

☒	Question	Why this matters
☐	7.1.9 Can I move from one backup product to another?	Yes – although it might be hard. Many backup products use the same format for the data on tape – this means that a backup tape created by one system can be read by another (hurray). However… the backup catalog will probably be proprietary. Many backup vendors have tools to help migration from other (competing) products to their own – so don't use the excuse that it is too hard… it is possible to move. A new supplier should be willing to help you migrate existing backups into the new system or enable parallel running while the new one takes over.
☐	7.1.10 How long have you supported product X?	When talking to a supplier, ask them how long they have supported a particular application. If they have been with it for years, this is good news – if they chop and change every year to different applications then they probably won't want to be someone you build a relationship with.
☐	7.1.11 What happens to my backups if I upgrade the operating system?	When you upgrade, you don't want the backups to become incompatible! This is almost always the case, sometimes an OS upgrade will lose support for a particular (old) tape drive or library – but the tapes should be compatible with new ones. For Windows systems, the use of dissimilar hardware restore functionality will mean that, only the appropriate data is restored, rather than all of it – causing the system to crash, or be unable to boot. A supplier should be able to offer help when it comes to upgrades of all types. Hopefully they will have read all the small print on incompatibilities and potential issues before you upgrade – but make sure you ask. As with most things in IT, it's better not to be the guinea pig.

☒	Question	Why this matters
☐	7.1.12 Do I need a dedicated backup network?	No. For the vast majority of companies, they use the same network for backup as for everyday traffic. However, some companies find that a dedicated network is useful to ensure that the main network is not impacted by ongoing backups and restores. A supplier should be able to quickly assess your needs and will probably offer a number of alternative solutions – one of which may be to have a separate network, especially if you have network load issues or a lot of data.
☐	7.1.13 What are the most computers/ systems I can backup?	More than you have! OK, so that sounds flippant, but the biggest backup domains (from a single master server) can have thousands of servers and tens of thousands of smaller clients. Multiple domains can be joined together to create a vast backup environment. Think of the biggest company you can – and they will have a backup system in place. Pick a supplier who is used to working with your size of organization. Ask for references.
☐	7.1.14 What's the least number of systems I can backup?	One! Backup applications can be used from a single machine up to global companies. You wouldn't necessarily use the same for both – smaller environments require less technically advanced backup applications, which can be easily administered by non-IT people. There is a backup solution for everyone. You shouldn't need any help in installing a single product backup system – unless you buy the wrong one.

☒	Question	Why this matters
☐	7.1.15 How big can a backup catalog get?	When a backup is taken, the information regarding the backup is stored in a catalog – things like which files (with their date stamps etc) are on which tape and so on. In a system which has millions of files, this catalog can become huge – several hundred gigabytes is not uncommon. Of course, this catalog also needs to be protected (backed up) – just in case it gets lost or corrupted. Catalogs can be recreated by reading the backup media, but it could be incredibly time consuming… If your supplier gets a little jittery with this question, it probably means they haven't done many actual installations. Ask for examples for companies which are similar in size to yours. When it comes to finding similarly sized companies, number of systems to be backed up and the number of files is a good start.

7.2 Implementing a solution

Choosing a backup solution is only one half of the problem. The other side is for either you or your supplier to get it installed, configured and up and running.

This next set of questions will help you understand whether the supplier is the one to help you with this task.

☒	Question	Why this matters
☐	7.2.1 How do you plan capacity in a backup system?	There are a number of utilities which backup vendors provide to help calculate what is needed. In essence, you enter data into a spreadsheet – how many servers, how much data, how often to be backed up and it then spits out a series of options for what you could use. For example how many tape drives or how much disk space. This becomes more complex when looking at utilizing de-duplication technologies, but again there are utilities to help with the planning. From the perspective of selecting a supplier, there is nothing like experience. Ask to see other estimates they have made and how they have turned out. While companies are very different in what they do, when it comes to backup it is possible to successfully work to a template.
☐	7.2.2 Do you have / use a backup coverage tool?	These tools are provided by backup vendors to look at which parts of your IT environment are backed up and which are not. They could be seen as a cynical selling tool, but actually they are very helpful in identifying where new systems or storage have been added but are not part of the backup.
☐	7.2.3 Do you have a backup migration service?	If you already have different backup applications in your organization you may need help in consolidating them. Rather than lose your existing backup data see if it is possible to migrate it. It's not the end of the world if you can't, you can always run multiple systems in parallel for a while – a pain, but not beyond the realms of possibility.

☒	Question	Why this matters
☐	7.2.4 What do I do to add a new machine to my backups?	Part of commissioning new systems, whether they are laptops or servers, should be to add it to a backup schedule. This may involve installing a backup application, or enabling one that is pre-installed as part of the company build. Often the new system will have to be verified to the backup application. If this is made part of the commissioning process then it won't be forgotten. Trusting to a new process is not ideal. Commissioning in a crisis often results in short-cuts, with the promise to come back and finish it later – but other things then take priority and so it never happens. Running coverage scripts on a regular basis will indicate where there may be holes in the backup environment. These can be run automatically, or it could be done as part of a Disaster Recovery (DR) test.
☐	7.2.5 Is all data equally important?	That depends… do you think all the data is equally important to you? The answer is usually 'no'. For this reason different backup strategies can be created so that more important (high business value) data is backed up more frequently, or perhaps with more copies than that which is of less importance.
☐	7.2.6 How do I classify my data?	There are a number of ways you can classify your data – the first is based on the value to your business and the second on sensitivity. So, financial plans and new product designs may be top secret and need to be backed up to a 'gold' standard, but equally, customer data, especially if it involves credit card or bank account details – while not so commercially top secret, also has to have the 'gold' standard due to data leak considerations.

☒	Question	Why this matters
☐	7.2.7 What's the toughest part about setting up a backup environment?	Getting started, especially if you have a relatively large network to begin with. Locating the most important servers and applications gives a good place to start – and can help minimize the initial cost. Backup environments tend to grow organically, so a phased approach can easily be taken.
☐	7.2.8 What's the biggest problem with backup environments?	Strangely, the biggest problem is usually that nothing (important) is backed up – and you don't find out until you come to restore it and nothing comes back. It is very easy to mis-configure a backup to miss backing up the important stuff or the important systems. For this reason coverage tools exist. When installing a backup solution, make sure the supplier tests that the backups work… completing a restore every so often will help increase faith in the system, so that in the event of a disaster, your first thought isn't… *Oh, I wonder if the backup worked…*
☐	7.2.9 Can I backup an open file?	The answer your potential supplier should give is *yes*. It tends to be an option and is most commonly used on laptops and desktops where important files are open when a backup occurs.

☒	Question	Why this matters
☐	7.2.10 What's an open file?	An open file is one which the application is still using. For example, on a laptop if you are editing a document, then that file is *open*. If the backup ran while you are editing the file, then it would not be backed up. Traditional backup solutions cannot backup open files – but there are solutions out there which can.
☐	7.2.11 Tell me about encryption.	This isn't so much a question as a statement. The supplier should understand both the plusses and the minuses of encryption – and not be allowed to escape from the question with an *Oh yes, the software handles that* type of answer.
☐	7.2.12 Why is encryption important?	Encryption is important to keep your data safe from prying eyes! Backup tapes, or CD ROMs don't have security built into them – you can read them on any drive, so anyone who found them could read your data! Encryption ensures that even if someone did find your backups, the data they contain would be safe. In these days of legislation and regulatory compliance. If the backups are going offsite at any point, then the data should be encrypted to keep it safe from becoming front page news as a data loss story.
☐	7.2.13 Why doesn't everyone use encryption?	Firstly, encryption wasn't deemed necessary all that long ago – if you lost a backup tape nobody worried! Secondly encryption causes a processing overhead – it is much slower to encrypt the data than not. Finally, if data in encrypted, then someone (i.e. you) has to look after the encryption keys and keep them safe – otherwise your data will be lost to you forever.

☒	Question	Why this matters
☐	7.2.14 How do I look after encryption keys?	Carefully. If encryption keys are lost you will never recover your data – and so might as well not have done the backup in the first place. Backup applications that use encryption manage the keys for you and make it easy for you to backup the keys as well!
☐	7.2.15 What do you do with encrypted files?	If you backup an encrypted file – which isn't part of the encryption system (for example an individual encrypts particular files) then you can end up with problems should you be (legally) asked for the data – and you can't decrypt the file. These encrypted files can be detected and reported on, or they can be excluded from the backup. A corporate policy should be put in place to deal with files which have been encrypted by an individual, either by banning the practice or requiring that the key be handed over, or a corporate solution is used.
☐	7.2.16 Should I have my data encrypted on the tapes?	Yes, the data should be encrypted if the tapes are going offsite – even if it is going between sites. Having said that, ideally the data won't be encrypted for long term storage – as you then don't have to worry about the encryption keys when it comes to restoring the data.

☒	Question	Why this matters
☐	7.2.17 Should I encrypt data 'across the wire'?	Encryption can be used at several points in the backup system; on tape (or media) is the obvious place. The other one is 'across the wire', which is when data is transferred from the backup client to the media server. This is useful if you have very sensitive information within an organization that you don't want to be snooped, or if you are backing up across the Internet. Encrypting across the wire can slow data transmission, but this can be offset by increasing multiplexing. The other plus is that the data can be decrypted before it is stored making it easier to restore.
☐	7.2.18 Can I backup a virtual machine?	Yes. In essence a virtual machine is one large blob of data – so backing it up is quite simple.
☐	7.2.19 Do you support virtual machine images and granular restore?	When talking to vendors about virtual machine backup, one important question is whether they can extract and restore a single file from within a complete virtual machine, without having to restore the whole machine. If not, then the recovery process will take longer and be more complex that you probably require.
☐	7.2.20 Can you restore a single file from a virtual machine backup?	Yes, there is technology for doing this for Microsoft® Exchange, Active Directory®, and SQL in a virtual environment with integrated VMware and Microsoft Hyper-V backup protection for virtual applications. Restoring individual files from a virtual machine without this technology is tough – if you don't want to restore the whole machine. Granular restore technology exists to make this easier and enable a single file to be extracted from a virtual machine image.

☒	Question	Why this matters
☐	7.2.21 Can you manage my backup environment for me?	If your supplier has installed your backup system for you, then they might well be able to run it for you as well. If this is what you want, then the question needs to be asked!
☐	7.2.22 How much time will it take to manage my backup environment?	This is useful to know whether you are going to run the system or a third party is. Is this a set-and-forget environment, or will it need time to be looked after every day? It might be that the only thing you need to do is take a tape or disk drive home each day, but that is still maintenance – so getting a list of the jobs that have to be done will help in working out the costs.
☐	7.2.23 Can you help with a disaster recovery plan?	Backup is just a part of a disaster recovery plan. A supplier who can help with installation and configuration of a backup system might also be able to help with a disaster recovery plan. This needs to include more than just the data from backup, it need to include resourcing new hardware as well as potentially temporary premises for the IT and personnel.

7.3 Questions for a Potential Internet Backup Service Provider

Time and technology has moved on and there are now a slew of service providers who can provide backup over the Internet. This isn't just for really small companies, but it is increasingly becoming an option for mid-sized enterprises as well.

As with anything new, there are still a few creases to be ironed out, but with a few smart questions you can make the right choice for your organization. The next set of questions are specific to service providers, however many of the questions in the previous sections are also worth asking – just how do they do their backups, how technologically advanced are they? If you already have a backup solution, ensure that they are doing at least as well as you are – and remember that cost isn't everything. If you can't get to your data when you need it, then your business will suffer.

☒	Question	Why this matters
☐	7.3.1 Can I backup over the Internet?	Some suppliers are now starting to offer Internet based backup services – you are connected to the Internet after all, so why not backup across it as well!
☐	7.3.2 What's the benefit of using backup over the Internet?	Ease-of-use! In essence you have just outsourced the backup service to someone else – they look after the data and manage the required infrastructure. You just pay for what you use, or a flat fee – making it a cost-effective alternative to doing it yourself.
☐	7.3.3 What's the disadvantage to backing up over the Internet?	There are two basic concerns – the first is security. Who has access to your data? The second is availability – will you have access to your data?
☐	7.3.4 Who has access to my data?	In traditional IT systems the systems administrator has complete control and privileges over everything – including being able to see all the data. While this is fine in-house, you may feel differently about a 3rd party being able to see your information. In order to overcome this issue, several service providers encrypt the data before it leaves your premises – and you are the only one with the encryption key. Just make sure you don't lose that key!

☒	Question	Why this matters
☐	7.3.5 What is the availability of my data?	When will you be having a disaster? You don't know… so you therefore need access to your data 24x7… 365 days a year. Some service providers have outages for maintenance, ensure you understand how often their service will be down (for whatever reason) before committing your data to the service. You should look to find one which has multiple copies of your information, held in more than one location – so if they have a disaster, it doesn't become your disaster as well.
☐	7.3.6 Can I see your disaster recovery plans?	If you are using a service, then you would no doubt hope that their disaster recovery plans are at least as good as yours, and hopefully better! If they don't have DR plans, then it is time to search for a new service provider…
☐	7.3.7 Can I audit your systems?	If you are using a service provider, then you would like to think that they do at least as much to secure and control their environment as you do – and the only way to check that is to audit them.
☐	7.3.8 Do you provide a report I can use with my auditors?	In these days of compliance legislation, being able to report that data is properly handled is extremely important. It may be impractical to audit a service provider – so they should produce a report you can use to satisfy your auditors.

☒	Question	Why this matters
☐	7.3.9 What are the costs associated with the service?	There are a number of different cost plans in use – and it will really depend on what you think you will need. Some services charge a fixed about per GB for storage per month, while others may charge for restoring information – either in terms of numbers of files, or bandwidth used. Remember, a service provider will have a fixed amount of bandwidth, and if it is heavily used, then the recovery of your data could take a long time.
☐	7.3.10 Can I use you as a primary backup service?	This is where all your backup data is stored and managed by the service provider. With the right security and availability, this is a great option for smaller companies.
☐	7.3.11 Can I use you as a secondary backup service?	This is where a portion of backup is stored online – perhaps instead of using tape. Several backup products now offer the opportunity to define a tier of storage as the Internet. This can provide peace of mind to medium sized companies, who also want a copy of the data in-house.

Funny you should say that

If one is only to talk from first-hand experience, conversation would be a very poor business.

CS Lewis (Author, 1898 - 1963)

BACKUP sounds like something that you should be doing, but haven't up until now – probably because you haven't had the need and therefore the inclination to do it. This Chapter aims to bring backup to life, with some real world stories. It might seem that most of these are here to spread fear, uncertainty and doubt (FUD), and it's true some of them are a little scary, and might make you think "there but for the grace…", but that's just it, backup is there to help when there is a problem. In some of these stories it's a case of "just in the nick of time" and those are the best ones. Someone has bought the software and implemented it just before a disaster struck and so they could recover quickly… in some cases, they could recover. Full stop. Something they wouldn't have been able to do at all without backup. Perhaps there should be a survey of companies who disappeared because they didn't have a backup…

If we'd interspersed these stories with the questions it would have made the last Chapters too long. It would also have prevented you

using the questions as checklists or aide-memoires. So we've grouped together our list of stories in this Chapter. I'm sure that you have your own stories – both positive and negative - so let us know them:

stories@Smart-Questions.com

8.1 Laptops and Large Magnets

So Employee "A" (a long since left, VP at Symantec as it happens) is sitting there playing with astoundingly powerful magnet right next to their computer with a pile of hard drives in it all whirring away. Not far away, a nice 19 inch monitor sits patiently waiting to be permanently wrecked if the shadow mask gets magnetized. Of all the things that people know you're not meant to ever do, our employee is probably doing it right now.

Hard drives and floppy disks store data with tiny magnetic spots on the media. When the read-head passes over these "spots" it reads the space as either "1" or "0". By placing a magnet next to the client media (not DVDs because they're optical), the "spots" will be altered, either by turning them all to "1" or all to "0" (depending on the polarity of the magnet), wherever the magnetic field reaches. The field has to be pretty strong to do damage, which is why small magnets are ok to be close to laptops.

Needless to say, the oversize magnet was then put on top of the laptop when it was put into its bag and lo and behold, when the laptop re-emerged it would no longer boot. The employee hadn't meant to stuff up their machine, but sometime *interesting stuff*, in this case a large magnet, gets in the way of common sense – and disasters, albeit small ones, occur.

If you're fortunate enough to be running a desktop or laptop backup product even if you do set fire to your PC in the most bizarre way possible you're safe in the knowledge that you can recover from losing the PC. Had the employee backed up their laptop and their work? Well, actually, they usually can't remember. Thank goodness for policy based management! Administrators simply force us all to do what we should be doing anyway.

So the last block level backup from the employee's laptop was the morning of their unfortunate game of death with the magnet, and according to the backup agent, the last backup was completed successfully, so they didn't lose much after all.

PS This reminds me of a medical researcher, who used to find their bank ATM cards would stop after about two days after receiving them… finally the bank asked and the answer was that they were in and out of CAT scanners (huge magnets) with their wallet in their back pocket… magnet, card magnetic stripe… card stops!

8.2 Almost a Disaster: 1

A small company had installed a laptop backup system along with full-disk encryption. It had been running for two years and it was time for the renewal... always tough when you're small and budgets are being squeezed.

The day before the license was due to expire, it really was the day before, they lost a laptop (it was taken from the back seat of his car while he was paying for petrol). Not a huge disaster on the face of it – however, this was enough to tip the scales, the renewal went through for two reasons:

- The individual was up and running by the end of the day, with a new laptop and all their data restored. (They lost the edits on one file!)
- The laptop contained customer data – but it wasn't a data leak as it was encrypted.

A quick calculation on the costs had they not been backed up had estimated that the loss of productivity for the person would have paid for the renewal, in essence they thought it would have been a week or so of his time – so it was their annual salary + bonus divided by 52.

They also tried to estimate the costs of a data loss event, but gave up very quickly when it became apparent that it would have been a crippling cost.

8.3 Almost a Disaster: 2

While there are a lot of examples of floods and fires, theft is probably the most common *disaster* that happens.

In this particular instance, it wasn't a laptop that was taken, but instead a data center that was targeted. The thieves were not after the servers, but the storage – the disk arrays. Storage is expensive and while the thieves must have had somewhere to sell the hardware on to, the saving grace was the backup.

The data center was replicated, but they needed to spin up replacement hardware as quickly as possible and the backup was the fastest way to do this – as well as keeping the new data safe while the replica was being initiated.

In 1993, The World Trade Center suffered its first bombing. The subsequent closure of the building turned out to be catastrophic for a number of businesses who hadn't put a Disaster Recovery or Business Continuity plan into place. For others, specifically some of the financial institutions who did have two data centers, realized that while they were prepared, previous disaster (floods, power outages etc) meant that they could get back to the building – in this case, if they hadn't been able to go back, then they would have been left with a single point of failure – which if that had failed with a simple disaster would have left them out-of-business. They also realized that it was not just IT that needed to work in the event of a disaster, it was the whole company. When the 2001 terrorist attacked occurred, it caused a catastrophic loss of life, but the companies continued.

The moral of the story is... if all you have is your data, then you won't be up and running, you need a comprehensive disaster recovery plan which includes hardware, software, personnel ***and*** the all-important data.

8.4 Accidentally Deleted Emails

There are only two types of Windows administrator. Those who have lost Microsoft Exchange data or those who are about to!

Some people delete their emails to avoid increasing the size of their Inbox; some people keep everything, just in case. Some people leave stuff sitting on the exchange server and some put things into PST files. Some people even have some form of archiving solution that solves some of the issues associated with loosing emails. Occasionally, and more often than you would think, an email gets deleted for which there is no backup. Problem.

A mid-sized organization based in a capital city in Europe had such an issue. To make matters worse this particular email was a critical sales request to their business, one of those *once-in-a-lifetime* opportunities – which sales people claim to have every day! Email deleted and Outlook shut down (the "delete all emails in the recycling folder on exit" policy was unfortunately set to "on").

The email had come into the organization during the early evening, been stored on the Exchange server from around 7 pm through to the deletion at 9.56 am. The messaging infrastructure and business file and print servers appeared to be separated by the red sea, so was the organization's backup strategy *good enough*? Their mid-sized business were still reliant on dedicated IT equipment and as a consequence had several small-scale backup solutions … all from different vendors (eight to be precise) were in place. It transpired that the Exchange server had been backed-up the night before – good news… but the administrator who knew all about that particular solution was on vacation – bad news. The company had to get in a consultant (we all know what that can cost – bad news) to recover the email – good news. Sadly, in the quest for a speedy recovery of the required item, they had to delete the existing data and roll back the Exchange system to the night before and then try and reconstitute what had happened following the restore – really bad news.

The moral of the story is: State-of-the-art is a moving goal. New backup technologies such as granular recovery improves productivity all round with the ability to restore a single email without having to restore (roll back) the entire system. Selected emails can be returned without affecting everyone and without requiring duplicate environments (which is the way some larger companies used to tackle the problem).

After the incident the company took a close look at their backup practices and realized that important business information now resided more on laptops and desktops rather than on servers, especially in their two remote offices. They were backing up data all over the place, but not any of the really important data – there was no solution for desktops and laptops (which had grown by 250% in recent years).

Different solutions managed in a different ways meant that it had become impossible to tell what was being backed up and what wasn't and recovery was inconsistent at best and not viable in too many cases. Understanding where their company data actually resided enabled them to develop requirements for a new backup system. They eventually implemented a single backup and recovery solution with special attention paid to geographically isolated end-users; desktops and remote devices; and to deal with the rapid growth in the volume of unstructured data.

8.5 Active Directory Disaster

Microsoft Active Directory (AD) as the primary directory service in Microsoft Windows with Microsoft Exchange, SQL, and SharePoint all dependent on efficient backup and quick recovery of AD. If you have any of these business applications you should be thinking about how you backup, and more importantly, restore AD as AD data corruption can have a disastrous affect across the Windows environment. The corruptions tend to come from accidental modification or deletion or faulty scripts accidentally overwriting key attributes.

AD is a replicated database; good for resiliency in the event of a failure but an accidentally deleted user account is immediately replicated and so can result in a lengthy process while someone struggles to recover the AD environment. This results in lost user productivity up to several hours, or even days. Unfortunately, the effects are not always immediately obvious...

And this is what happened to one organization that discovered that AD had dropped some user attributes. (OK, so it was user error – as they were changing some items across multiple accounts – and things don't magically disappear... *"I didn't do anything, honest guv just did what I usually do."*) The majority of those affected were sales reps who were on the road, so it didn't become clear what had happened for several hours by which time a good deal of damage had already occurred.

The data needing to be backed up had grown to the point where a backup which included individual AD objects was taking nearly 24 hours - so could only be done at the weekend. Rather than look at new technology, they decided the risk was ok and so would just do a complete backup once a week. This meant they had no choice but to do an all or nothing recovery of AD… which was pretty painful and took down the Microsoft server environments for a day.

As with most backup stories, there is often a dawning realization after an event (aka disaster), and here they realized that Microsoft's dependence on AD meant that they really needed to revisit the AD backup solution.

They chose a solution with new technology which enabled a single pass fast backup but with granular recovery technology giving them the ability to restore individual AD items, including individual user accounts.

It's useful to use other people's experience to your own benefit, when you hear of a (disaster) story ask whether something similar could happen in your organization – and the brush off of *"oh, it won't happen to us"* is not useful!

8.6 Lightning never strikes Twice

The threat of data loss exists with almost every click of your mouse. Life in the online world can be dangerous.

A reasonably large engineering organization (mainly CAD design) based in London, had a good disaster recovery (DR) plan. They tested it every 6 months and it worked. From a backup perspective, they ran a backup to a tape library and before they sent the tapes off-site they recovered the data from the newly backed up tape. All good, so far.

But... (there is always a *but* in these case studies)... they had a couple of pieces of really bad luck. Firstly the server room was on the top floor of a two story building and the second was that although they had carried out a recovery test with tapes fresh from a backup, they never tried it with a tape from the off-site store.

One dark and stormy night lightning struck their building and everything in their server room became toast in the fire that broke out. After the initial shock, their DR plan kicked in and before they knew it the new servers arrived at their DR site.

The General Manager organized the retrieval of the latest off-site tape and a courier dutifully turned up on time and at the right place. Nothing on the tape. So they got another one, and another one, and another one – all blank. Eventually they sent a van to pick up a number of tapes – when they were delivered they managed to restore from the first tape they used. Everyone was flummoxed. How come when they had sent the courier across London and back the tapes were blank and when they came back on a van, hey presto, there was all the data? Of course, the other tapes were over three days old (tapes from day 1, 2, & 3 were blank).

What had happened was that the courier had travelled across the city by Underground. He would stand *in the right place for the doors* and put his bag and the tape on the floor – which happened to be right over the train's electric engine … unfortunately the engine's electromagnetic field interfered with the magnetic tape... no more data.

They lost several days of work, from the disaster and then having to re-do work that had already been done.

The moral of this story is to always test in as completely realistic environment as possible – testing every step of the chain. They also realized that DR planning was tough and they should have had more than one copy of the backup data. In the short term, they instigated tape duplication, so one copy stayed onsite (in a fireproof safe) while another was stored offsite. They are now looking at using backup to disk onsite (for speed) with tapes then being created without impacting the production systems and stored offsite.

Final Word

History is merely a list of surprises. It can only prepare us to be surprised yet again.

Kurt Vonnegut (American Novelist, 1922 – 2007)

BACKUP is an essential part of any modern business. We rely on electronic data to keep our businesses going, when it stops flowing, so does the business. Unfortunately events often interrupt the flow of data and that's where backup comes in. It's like an insurance policy – but once you have it, you will wonder how you did without it!

New technologies and work practices have meant that state-of-the-art backup applications have had to move with the times in order to support the new ways of working. This means there are a lot of possibilities for you when it comes to implementing a backup solution in your organization – which is good and bad. If there was only one, then the decision making process would be greatly simplified, but as it is you need to understand your IT environment and your requirements. For very small businesses, a backup solution can be introduced over a weekend and no-one will necessarily know it's there. For others, the planning will take longer and the implementation will have to be phased in over the course of a few weeks.

You are going to need a plan in order to succeed:

- Start with finding information on websites from the major backup application providers, such as Symantec www.symantec.com who have a number of backup products and can provide a solution to fit any size of organization.
- Talk to friends and colleagues, there is nothing like a personal recommendation on a product or group buy-in for the idea to gain confidence in what you are doing.
- Read magazine articles and product reviews.
- Download a trial copy of some software and give it a try.

The good news is that you can start small and grow the environment just as efficiently as if you do it all at once. So, put backup at the top of the list of things to do today and get the ball rolling – you won't regret it.

Notes pages

Notes pages

Notes pages

Lightning Source UK Ltd.
Milton Keynes UK
28 September 2010

160471UK00001B/2/P